SOFTWARE UNDER SIEGE:
VIRUSES AND WORMS

E.L. Leiss

*Department of Computer Science
and Research Computation Laboratory
University of Houston, Texas, USA*

Elsevier Advanced Technology
Mayfield House, 256 Banbury Road, Oxford OX2 7DH, UK
Commissioned by
Technical Communications (Publishing) Ltd

British Library Cataloguing in Publication Data
Leiss, Ernest L., 1952-
    Software under siege.
    1. Computer systems. Viruses. Management aspects
    I. Title
    658.4'78

    ISBN 0-946395-58-6

ii

PREFACE

Computer viruses have recently attracted widespread attention, all of it negative. Although they had been known at least since 1983, they were customarily dismissed as insignificant and posing no discernable threat. Subsequent successful attacks by viruses and similar attackers have disproved this position, with the result that parts of the computing community have now embraced the other extreme, a great deal of fear and loathing and a distinct feeling of defenselessness.

This book is based on the premise that a known enemy is easier to defeat than an unknown one. To this end we describe various methods of attacking computer systems and draw conclusions from then about ways of combatting viruses. We feel that there are many who are not interested in all technical intricacies of viruses, but nevertheless want to obtain a reasonably accurate and complete description of the threat posed by them. Thus, we have avoided using too much technical jargon. For those readers who do want to learn more about the technical details, we have included references which should satisfy their interest in more technical points.

This book grew out of an article on computer viruses that I was asked to prepare for the 1990 yearbook of the Encyclopedia of Physical Science and Technology. Subsequently, I felt the need for a more in-depth treatment of this topic, which eventually occasioned the present book. In collecting literature for these works, I was ably assisted by a graduate student, Ms. I-Ling Yen; of course any omissions and errors are exclusively my own fault. By and large, this book reflects the status of virus research and related developments through summer 1989. It is therefore very up-to-date at the time it goes to press and should provide an accurate reflection of developments in this field.

E.L. Leiss

CONTENTS

PART III DIAGNOSIS 61

Chapter

PART IV PREVENTION AND CURES 75

Chapter

PART I

INTRODUCTION

The introduction sketches the backdrop against which the threats against data integrity are played out. It discusses changes in the way computing is done and their relationship to the emerging threats by computer viruses and other attackers.

Chapter One

Background: Changes and Concerns

This book is about computer viruses, worms, logical bombs, and other threats to software and data. It will describe the illness, starting with actual attacks, define the causes, and discuss diagnosis as well as possible cures and prevention. However, in order to understand the phenomenon better, one has to start with the overall context within which these problems were able to arise.

Our starting point is an incident, of which certain facts are clear and well known. On the evening of November 2, 1988, a piece of software attacked and successfully invaded an estimated 6000 computer systems world-wide. Within a matter of hours, these systems were inoperable. Reportedly, this was the first time that mainframes were attacked; prior to this incident, only personal computers (PCs) had been affected in several relatively isolated instances. The November 2, 1988, incident exploded the myth that only rather unsophisticated systems such as PCs were vulnerable, thereby creating a great deal of anxiety in commercial computing centers around the world.

Instead of asking how computer virus attacks can occur, it proves much more instructive to ask why there were no extensive attacks earlier. The answer to this question lies in the change that occurred in computing in general in the last five years or so.

1.1 Changes in Computing Milieu

Several major changes occurred in the way users view computing in the past few years. Two of these are of central interest in our exploration of the reasons why

3

viruses and other attackers threaten the security and integrity of our computer installations. The first relates to the way in which computing is, and has been, administered; it reflects the trend away from monolithic, hierarchical computing centers or centralized computing and towards networks of local workstations or distributed computing. The second change has to do with the distribution of software, in particular the sharing of software at a variety of levels.

1.1.1 Centralized versus Decentralized Computing

Until the beginning of the 1980s, most serious computing was done on mainframes. Together with this came a certain mindset: there was a centralized computing center; all processing power was located there; virtually all data and all programs were stored there; users submitted jobs, typically for batch processing, from (dumb) terminals; and most importantly, all systems programmers were physically located at this center. As a result, any user who needed capabilities that were not ordinarily granted to end users had to submit a request to the computing center which in turn acted upon it. Thus, systems privileges were tightly restricted to a rather small group of systems programmers who could be rather stringently controlled, both physically and organizationally (see Figure 1).

Interactive processing became commercially accepted in the 1970s; in principle it gave the end user more capabilities, but the mindset did not change substantially. However, interactive computing did force the operating systems to become more sophisticated since now several users were active at the same time; consequently safeguards had to be built in to protect users that were running jobs at the same time from interfering with each other.

At the end of the 1970s, PCs made their appearance. Initially these were very primitive systems. Designed for a single user, they were slow, with insufficient data storage and very rudimentary operating systems. By and large, these were home computers, as opposed to business computers, and they remained just that, even when individual systems became more powerful. In advertisements and computer magazines, PCs were quite early touted as superior to terminals connected to central mainframes; however the business community remained largely unconvinced. For good reason: most business activities tend to be interrelated; different units of the same enterprise must operate on a common database. Consequently, computers that were unable to share data and programs efficiently and consistently did not meet the requirements of business data processing in the 1980s. (Copying data onto floppy disks and sharing disks should be viewed akin to corresponding by pigeon carriers.) Moreover, secondary data storage facilities of PCs were simply inadequate for business purposes.

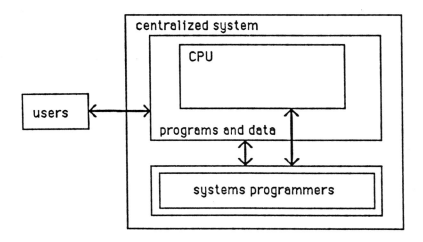

Figure 1. Centralized processing

This situation changed substantially with the advent of networking, especially local area networks (LANs), in the second half of the 1980s. Instead of having isolated islands (read PCs) floating independently in a sea of information, accessing data independently and producing possibly inconsistent results, all computers of an enterprise could now be connected to each other, including PCs and mainframes. Even more importantly, through the use of networks data storage could be organized so that different processors could access the same databases and operate on them in a consistent manner.

With networking came a decentralization of power, as the computing center personnel were no longer the undisputed high priests of computing in a company. Most other units in a commercial enterprise would have fought such a development. For example, accounting functions are typically reasonably centralized, reporting to a controller, who would strenuously oppose any move to distribute these functions to the smallest operational units (departments, project teams) of a company. However, since personal work stations (as PCs came to be known, once marketing divisions of PC manufacturers realized that businesses did not want to buy PCs - read home computers - for their employees) and networking were considered the cutting edge of computing technology, computing centers either acquiesced to, or even became active champions of, the decentralization of computing.

This development implied a rather subtle but from our point of view crucial change: every employee who had a work station on his or her desk now acquired, to some extent, functions that previously were carried out by systems programmers. While in many cases this change was not obvious to the user, since it rarely went beyond the loading of the operating system which for most employees was not much more than the switching on of the terminal, at the operational level this introduced a qualitative and most important difference: it was now the end user that was in control of the computer, and not the computing center personnel (see Figure 2).

6

BACKGROUND

The significance of this shift did not become immediately apparent to the users, nor for that matter to most computing center directors. However, at the level of the operating system, it had far reaching consequences. As we pointed out, the systems software (file systems, operating systems, etc.) of PCs was basically designed with a single user in mind. As soon as PCs were connected to each other (and to mainframes), this single-user world view was shattered; yet the operating systems of many personal work stations did not change drastically: on the one hand, networking was added to enhance the functionality of the older systems, on the other hand, even newer systems sometimes ran older systems software, usually for reasons of compatibility. As a result, safeguards against (accidental or malicious) undesired changes of data and software were, and still are, substantially inadequate. Since most networks are not safe (and are really not designed to be safe), it is the processors on which the burden of safeguarding data and software rests. For historical reasons as well as for reasons of personnel management, mainframes are somewhat more resilient to such changes than personal work stations (but by no means impervious; see Section 4.4).

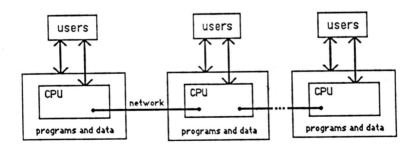

Figure 2. Processing using networked workstations.

1.1.2 Sharing of Software

With the advent of significantly expanded programmer communitites, the question arose whether it made sense to write programs for essentially the same problems again and again. This question was (obviously) answered negatively, and this gave rise to the problem of how to share software. Sharing here has a variety of meanings. It could be attempting to copy (usually illegally) a major piece of code supplied by a vendor with the objective of avoiding purchase; it could result from identifying an interesting and desirable technique for solving a particular common problem in a colleague's software; or it could be the consequence of a carefully designed "toolbox" of modules which a programmer established in order to simplify the task of solving complex problems. In all these cases, it is clear that both the person having the software and the person desiring it must agree to exchange the code. This is true regardless of whether the sharing involved is legal, i.e., if the owner has the right to make copies and distribute them, or not. Thus, in the situations described a certain personal relationship had to be established, a certain amount of trust was required.

A subtle change in this occurred with the advent of bulletin boards and program exchanges: the sharing became far less personal. In many cases, the person copying did not know the original owner of the software and guarantees were usually explicitly denied. However, these disclaimers were universally disregarded by the programmers who acquired at little or no cost interesting and attractive software that allowed them to do things that were either beyond their capabilities or would have required a substantial investment in time which they were unwilling to make.

In this way, trust was established that was misplaced, since it could be, and was, abused by more or less vicious pranksters. Programs were placed on electronic bulletin boards under the pretext of making them available to the general public whose primary function was the infection of the computer system on which they were installed. A particularly vicious (or ingenious) example is the program

Flu-Shot 4 which masqueraded as an anti-virus product but in fact was itself a damage-causing virus. Bulletin boards in this way provided an attacker with a trusted means of entry to a system, which was clearly in its ultimate result the antithesis to the purpose for which they were created; because they facilitated the distribution of attacks they undermined the very purpose for which they were created, namely the distribution and sharing of information and software.

Decentralized processing and software sharing provide the background against which the drama is played out. Many problems stemming from virus attacks can ultimately be traced back to this change in the computing milieu.

A related issue is that of convenience of use, which in most cases is compounded by the decentralization of control.

1.2   Protection versus Convenience of Use

Many security risks can be eliminated by using certain precautions. One problem with these precautions is that they almost invariably reduce the ease of use of the resulting system. For example, some of the threats to data integrity could be eliminated by encrypting data together with some redundancy (for more details, see the Appendix). The major drawback of this approach is that the data file must be decrypted before each use.

A more mundane example is the use of nontrivial passwords. As we will see, among others, the November 2 incident referred to above was substantially facilitated by the fact that users tend to choose rather simple passwords, which can often be guessed by an attacker. The obvious advantage of simple passwords is that they can be remembered easily. More complicated passwords tend to be written down and stored in an easily accessible location - thereby again compromising the security of the system they are supposed to protect. Note however that in the case of easily guessable passwords anybody with access to the network can become a threat, while in the case of passwords posted in a drawer or on the side of the work station, physical access to the employee's office is required before a threat may materialize. Since physical access to an office is traditionally more restricted than access to a general purpose data network, complicated passwords, even if they are posted on the terminal, may be more secure than simple passwords which can be easily remembered but also guessed.

The problem of convenience of use is aggravated by the decentralization of control; previously a computing center might have unilaterally assigned passwords and changed them periodically to other prespecified ones; now the owner of a work station is in control of this. While it would of course be possible to assign preselected passwords to all participants in a network (and to change them periodically), this clearly goes against the notion of a "personal work station" − and is therefore often not done.

Another variation on this theme is provided by short-cuts. These are methods that circumvent ordinary controls, designed to ensure privacy and integrity. In most cases these short-cuts are used for convenience, and again they provide attackers with a convenient means of penetrating systems. For example, in the November 2 incident the perpetrator took advantage of such a short-cut.

Taken together the changes in computing milieu and the related emphasis on ease of use of computing equipment provide an answer to our original question, namely why computer virus attacks had not occurred earlier: while the programming techniques used to design viruses were certainly known for quite some time, it was widespread networking together with the decentralization of control that provided the fertile soil in which computer viruses could flourish.

1.3 Potential for Damage

Before 1988, several minor incidents had hinted at a potential for major problems related to the organized and widespread subversion of computer systems, and most importantly the possibility of massive destruction of data and software. These concerns were considered by most to be rather remote possibilities. In 1988 however they spilled over into public awareness, primarily due to an incident which received front page coverage in both *The Wall Street Journal* and in *The New York Times*, two highly influential daily US newspapers.

The reason for the attention attracted by this incident lies in the potential for destruction of data pointed out by it. With the exception of certain installations related to defense matters and national security, many larger computer installations are today connected via computer networks to other installations. As outlined, PCs are now also increasingly networked together. Networks are in essence systems that allow the transmission of digitally encoded information (data, programs, messages) at relatively high speeds and in relatively convenient ways from one system to another. Subverting the proper functioning of a network may therefore result in the subversion of access controls in the computer systems that are linked together by the network. Consequently, a scenario is quite feasible whereby a program may be transmitted within a network that is capable of destroying large amounts of data in all those computer systems that it can reach in a network. The case that such a scenario is not only conceivable but in fact quite plausible had been made for a number of years, starting with Fred Cohen's demonstration of a computer virus in 1983. It was in 1988 that such a scenario was actually played out in a major and highly public way.

The economic implications of the destruction of large data volumes in a computer system hardly need be explained. Once this is multiplied by the number of systems involved in a network (in the November 2 incident, it was estimated that over 6000 installations were affected), the material consequences could be staggering. Indeed it is generally agreed that the loss of a substantial portion of a business's data may force it into bankruptcy. Furthermore, malfunctioning of a certain system due to missing data or programs may result in massive loss of life (e.g., an air traffic control system; a control system for a hydro-electric dam or a nuclear power plant). Equally important, the potential of disruption can also be damaging: a bomb threat can conceivably be more paralyzing than the explosion of a small bomb itself. While it is natural to call for protection against these threats, this may be impossible by purely technical means or at the very least only at unacceptably high costs, since any solution would drastically reduce the functionality or ease of use of the resulting system. As we pointed out, the notion of user-friendliness of a computer system or a communications network is frequently antithetical to the notions of data security and data integrity.

1.4 A Comment on Legal Issues

It is tempting to fight the threat of viruses by legal means. However, this is probably the most difficult approach. On the one hand, it is very difficult to arrive at legal language that addresses precisely the threat posed by viruses and similar attackers, and on the other hand such legislation will never be able to prevent attacks, only to punish them after they have occurred. It is probably very difficult if not impossible to differentiate legally between legitimate mail messages and the Internet attack described in more detail in Section 4.4 which also consisted of sending mail messages, just very many. (Is junk mail illegal?) Also, it should be noted that in order to prosecute, it must be possible to prove "beyond reasonable doubt" that a certain person perpetrated an attack. In this context one should note that there is definitely nothing illegal about possessing a virus (Chapter six expresses the view that there can never be anything illegal about it since one could not possibly have a general test of software to contain a virus). Thus, it would be necessary to prove beyond any reasonable doubt that someone released (wilfully, presumably) a virus. Also, if intent to do damage is to be a criterion, it will be very difficult to formulate it so that simple mistakes cannot cause a programmer to be criminally prosecuted. Civil suits may be more successful, as they are not subject to the same stringent proof rules; however, they also suffer from the same problem as criminal suits, namely that most suits can only be brought after a successful attack. Thus, they are reactive and not preventive. All these issues contribute to make it very unlikely that legal measures can be employed effectively to prevent attacks by viruses and the like.

1.5 Security and Integrity

In the preceding we have distinguished between security and integrity of a system. While the two terms are related, they are nevertheless quite different. We will briefly differentiate them here; the Appendix contains more details on several techniques related to security and integrity of data.

Data security deals with every type of unauthorized access to data or software in a computer system; data integrity on the other hand is concerned only with unauthorized changes or erasures of data and software. Thus, strictly speaking, data security is a more general notion. However, typically the emphasis is on read access, in contrast to integrity where it is write access that is of concern. Again, one can differentiate between outright destruction of data and the insidious change of data. Both play an important role for computer viruses, but in very different ways. The ability to make insidious changes is precisely what enables the virus to propagate itself from one system or account to the next. The ability to wantonly destroy data is the main threat of a computer virus. Loosely speaking, it is somewhat easier to prevent insidious changes than to prevent data vandalism, but the cost may in both cases be prohibitively high.

1.6 Bibliographical Notes

The development of computing related in most of this chapter is well known to computer professionals world-wide - most of the changes have occurred only in the last ten years or so. Fred Cohen's first demonstrations of computer viruses were reported in [1]; more accessible are the accounts given in [2] and [3]. The various incidents related to attacks on the integrity of computer systems that subsequently attracted the public's attention will be discussed in more detail in later chapters. The November 2, 1988, incident was featured on the front pages of two leading US newspapers, *The Wall Street Journal* ([4]; other related articles in this edition are [5] and [6], with [7] being an early reaction to the incident) and *The New York Times* ([8]). The extent to which the November 2, 1988, incident mesmerized the press (and presumably the public) can be gleaned from some reactions in non-technical publications: the monthly magazine *Discover* devoted almost three pages of its review of noteworthy events, discoveries, and inventions in the year 1988 to computer viruses ([9]), the highly respected weekly *Science News* had a detailed article about the November 2, 1988, attack ([10]), and the weekly magazine *Newsweek* reflected the concern about, and morbid fascination with, attacks on computers ([11]). (However, it should be emphasized that virus-like products may have useful purposes; see for example [12].) While earlier attacks had received some notice in daily newspapers (e.g., [13] and [14]), most of the expression of concern was carried out in more technical publications ([15]), if not at a more technical level ([16], [17], [18], [19], [20]). Concerns of insurance and coverage are reflected in [21]. Legal issues are addressed in [22] and [23]. Since then, attacks on computers have received more prominent and more rapid publication (e.g., [24], [25]), but the November 2, 1988, incident and its alleged perpetrator, Robert Tappan Morris, a Cornell University graduate student, still command some attention ([26], [27]). In [28] it was reported that Morris was suspended by Cornell through fall 1989; Cornell's Report has recently been released (see also [29]). In [30], it was reported that Morris was indicted by a U.S. federal grand jury on a felony computer crime charge for the release of the Internet Worm; this makes him the first person to be prosecuted under the 1986 Computer Fraud and Abuse Act.

PART II

THE ILLNESS

Part II describes what viruses, worms, and other attackers are, how they have evolved, and where they have occurred. It also describes other attacks and relates them to the main characters in our bestiary.

15

Chapter Two
Brief History of Computer Virus Attacks

In this chapter we briefly review some of the more important computer virus attacks that have occurred. As will become clear in the next chapter where we give reasonably formal definitions, there are several terms beside that of virus that are of interest. Therefore we will cast our net here somewhat wider and include several schemes for attack which are not computer viruses in a strict sense. Common to all of them is the characteristic that the threat comes from a piece of code, and not directly from a human being. For a case study of the latter, see Chapter 5.

2.1 Precursors of Viruses

One of the predecessors of computer viruses was a class of programs, designed at Xerox Palo Alto Research Center for a serious purpose, namely locating computers in a network which are idle at a certain point in time, in order to harness their processing power for 'background jobs' — computing tasks that require huge amounts of time but do not have a firm completion date and can therefore run whenever no other tasks are executing.

The motivation underlying the concept of background job is that there is little difference in cost between a computer that is operational but does not perform any computations and one that is used; therefore background jobs can be run practically for free. These programs, conceived around 1980, were called "worm" programs. Since they were to perform their objective without human intervention, they were designed to replicate themselves in idle machines so that a copy at such an idle machine could then become the starting point for further searches for idle machines in the network. Note that in contrast to typical computer viruses, each copy of the Xerox Palo Alto worms retained a complete list of all other copies; this clearly required that all copies had to stay in continual communication.

One important lesson of these early experiments was the realization that it was surprisingly difficult to control a worm running amok. In one instance, the only way to stop a worm that had accidentally been changed and was malfunctioning, thereby disabling the systems on the network (by clogging them with copies of itself), was to make use of an emergency escape which the designers had built into the worm mechanism. In the aftermath of this debacle (it left 100 computers 'dead'), the designers paid some attention to the question of what might cause a worm program to run amok. It should be noted that in contrast to a computer virus, which is designed to adversely affect computers, the Xerox Palo Alto worm programs were designed for a perfectly legitimate and definitely useful purpose; it was only when something went wrong that their proliferation shut the entire network down. The authors caution in their 1982 paper, which predates the first formulation of a computer virus, "that the development of distributed worm control algorithms with low delay and stable behavior is a challenging area". (See section 2.4 for reference). As subsequent developments indicate, this was a very prescient remark.

There were other programs with similarities to computer viruses that predate the Xerox Palo Alto worm programs. The same paper that describes the Xerox Palo Alto worm programs also mentions the 'Creeper', an auto-relocatable program designed in the early 1970s (by B. Thomas of Bolt, Beranek and Newman) to move autonomously through a major US research network (Arpanet), and an enhanced version (by R. Tomlinson) which had the additional ability to replicate itself. Again, the fact that it was found necessary to complement this program with one that would move through the network in an attempt to find and disable copies of the Creeper program can be considered (with hindsight) a disturbing omen of things to come.

Probably the most easily accessible and most widely read description of programs that are similar to computer viruses in that they self-replicate and destroy data is given by A. K. Dewdney in a series of columns on Computer Recreations in the popular magazine *Scientific American*. These articles refer to a game called Core War where hostile programs attempt to destroy each other by modifying information stored in core memory. There is a certain amount of irresponsibility involved, since the columns promote active programming efforts by the reader, and the potential for one of these core war programs to escape and wreak havoc is not insignificant.

2.2 Reported Virus Attacks

In this section we give a list of virus attacks that have been reported in the open literature. Although there is a tendency of victimized organizations to keep quiet about a computer virus attack, on balance it is unlikely that a major attack can be covered up, since by its very nature a successful virus will involve many users, and it is much more difficult to keep an attack a secret if the affected user group is large.

We divide this section into two parts; the first part deals with attacks on networks of PCs, the second one with attacks on mainframes.

2.2.1 PC Networks

A good number of attacks are known; we list some of them. We indicate what systems were affected, how the virus was introduced, and what damage was caused.

(a) *The Freehand Virus*. This virus affects the Apple Macintosh personal computer. Reportedly, it was inadvertently distributed by Aldus Corporation in the commercial graphics package 'Freehand'. It is instructive to trace out how this virus came into existence.

The Freehand virus was posted in an electronic bulletin board by a programmer, reportedly identified as living in the southwestern United States; it subsequently infected systems of a group of programmers located in Montreal, Canada, who are associated with the magazine *MacMag*. This group apparently copied the virus onto diskettes that were distributed at a users' conference, one of which was given to Macromind, Inc., a Chicago based company that distributes training diskettes. Aldus Corp. believes that the virus infiltrated its systems via a Macromind diskette.

It appears that the virus does not destroy data or files. It does replicate itself onto other, uninfected disks, then reads the internal clock. On March 2, 1988, the first anniversary of Apple's introduction of the Macintosh II PC, it caused the computer to print out an innocuous message. The virus then destroys itself.

(b) *The Lehigh Virus.* This virus affects personal computers running the PC-DOS and MS-DOS operating systems. It was first discovered in late 1987 at Lehigh University; its origin is unclear. It is a malicious virus which conceals itself in the operating system. It does this in a fairly sophisticated way so as to escape detection. Once it is triggered it attempts to replicate itself onto any other disk that contains an uninfected copy of the operating system. Each time it succeeds with an infection, it increases an internal counter by 1. When this counter reaches 4, the virus erases dictionary information on the disk which renders the entire disk unusable. While this virus is quite clever at concealing itself, its author overlooked that its insertion into the operating system updates the date of last change for the operating system file; this provides an indication of the presence of the virus.

This virus displays an important characteristic, namely delayed destruction, here accomplished by counting the number of infected operating systems. If the virus were to destroy immediately the disk on which it resides, its spread would be stopped very rapidly. Even if it destroyed the disk only after it infected another disk, users would be alerted instantaneously. As it is, the virus may lie seemingly dormant for a while, using this time to infect four other disks, and only then it makes one disk unusable.

(c) *The Pakistani or Brain Virus.* This virus also affects PCs running the DOS operating system. It was first reported at the University of Delaware and later, somewhat modified, at the universities of Pittsburgh and Pennsylvania as well as George Washington and Georgetown universities. Its second name derives from the fact that in the absence of a volume label on the infected floppy disk, it creates the volume label 'Brain'. The first name indicates the origin of the virus. Tracing the virus to Pakistan is not as much a masterpiece of detective work as one might think, since the virus contains the following embedded message:

"Welcome to the Dungeon, (c) 1986 Basit & Amjad (pvt) Ltd., BRAIN COMPUTER SERVICES..730 NIZAM BLOCK ALLAMA, IQBAL TOWN, LAHORE, PAKISTAN..PHONE: 430791,443248, 280530. Beware of this VIRUS.....Contact us for vaccination."

The brothers Basit and Amjad Alvi sell PCs; when contacted, Basit admitted having written the virus but both brothers could not explain how it infiltrated the USA. The virus caused considerable damage; at Delaware it infected several hundred student disks and made several completely unusable. Similar damage was reported at Pittsburgh.

(d) *The Hebrew University Virus.* This virus was detected at the Hebrew University in Israel. It was designed to spread, on every Friday and on the thirteenth of each month prior to Friday, May 13, 1988, to disks and programs resident on any of the university's 1000 microcomputers, used by students and faculty. Then, on Friday, May 13, 1988, it was to erase all files on all infected systems and disks. It was detected before the target date for destruction because a design flaw caused the virus to infect already infected disks, thereby greatly slowing down the individual systems and the network during the days when it replicated itself; also because of the unlimited replication, increasing amounts of memory were used by the copies of the virus thereby inadvertently alerting users to the virus's presence.

Again, we note the time delay feature which allows the virus to spread, in order to give it the chance to inflict maximum damage. We also note the design flaw, namely that already infected files are again infected; this is not the only instance where such a design flaw helped in discovering viruses.

As an interesting aside, we note that in addition to being considered an unlucky day by superstitious people, the target date is also the fortieth anniversary of the eve of Israel's declaration of independence (May 14, 1948).

(e) *The Amiga Virus.* As the name indicates, this virus affects the Amiga personal computer, produced by Commodore Corporation. It appeared first in England and Australia, and later infected an Amiga users group in Florida. Its origin is suspected to be a disk provided by Amiga distributors. The virus is malicious. It first copies itself from an infected disk into the RAM (random access memory) of the computer. Then it infects other disks. After a while, a message appears on the screen ("Something wonderful has happened - your machine has come alive"); after this, the computer is unable to execute any programs on the disk. The virus can be eliminated from the system by switching off the computer, as the virus resides in RAM which is erased during power loss.

(f) *The Flu-Shot 4 Virus.* This malicious virus is a particularly vicious prank which appeared on various computer network bulletin boards. It pretends to be an updated version of Flu-Shot 3, one of several virus detection programs. Flu-Shot 4 erases crucial dictionary information on the hard disk, thereby causing loss of data and files.

(g) *The IBM Christmas Tree Virus.* In December 1987, this virus, reportedly written by a West German student, infected IBM's internal communication network, with 250,000 users. It copied itself in chain letter fashion at least one half million times within two hours, but did not destroy data or files. It replicated itself by sending a copy of itself to every user who had exchanged mail with the virus's current host. Its only action consisted of printing on the screen a Christmas greeting and drawing a tree. The virus slowed the network down and IBM was reportedly able to purge it before it spread to systems of customers. Technically (see Chapter 3), it was a worm rather than a virus, since it was not permanently stored.

(h) *The Scores Virus.* This virus infected Apple Macintosh software at a variety of US government agencies over a period of five months. The virus was designed to

Name of Virus	Damage	Origin	Affected Systems	Delayed Action
Freehand	none/ message	commercial package	Macintosh	no
Lehigh	substantial	unknown	DOS systems	yes
Pakistani	substantial	Pakistan	DOS systems	no
Hebrew U.	extensive/ prior detection	unknown	various	yes
Amiga	some	England/ Australia (commercial package)	Amiga	yes
Flu-Shot 4	extensive	bulletin board		
IBM Xmas	none/ message	student	IBM systems	no
Scores	substantial	unknown	various	no

Figure 3. Summary of Some PC Viruses

23

sabotage programs at Electronic Data Systems, a large US software company, currently owned by General Motors Corporation. The affected agencies include the National Aeronautics and Space Agency (NASA; facilities in Washington, Maryland, and Florida), the Environmental Protection Agency (EPA), the National Oceanic and Atmospheric Administration (NOAA), and the US Sentencing Commission. The virus reportedly caused damage by crashing systems and destroying files, thereby delaying projects and requiring substantial efforts to track it down.

We summarize the various successful virus attacks on PCs together with their characteristics in Figure 3. Many of these viruses continue to affect users, either in their original version or as a modification. While a known virus can usually be detected and purged (see Section 7.4), these programs may not work for modifications.

2.2.2 Mainframe Attacks

On November 2, 1988, a program (technically it was a worm, not a virus) invaded an estimated 6000 computers linked together by a major US network called Internet, which includes Arpanet, Milnet, and NSFnet. Affected were computers running a version of the operating system Unix. The worm took advantage of two different flaws, namely a debugging device in the mail handler (which most computer sites left in place, even though it was not required any longer after successful installation) and a similar problem in a communications program. The worm exploited these flaws by causing the mail handler to circumvent the usual access control in a fairly sophisticated way; it also searched users' files for lists of trusted users (users with higher levels of authority) and used them to infiltrate other programs. Additionally, it attempted to guess passwords in order to infiltrate users.

The worm's means of transmission between computers was the network. Because infiltrated sites could be reinfiltrated arbitrarily often (clearly a design flaw of the worm), systems (especially those that were favorite

24

recipients of mail) became saturated and stopped performing useful work. This was how users discovered the infiltration, and this was also the primary damage the worm caused. We note that this was not the first time an infiltrator was detected because it kept infecting already infected sites and programs (cf. the Hebrew University Virus). The worm did not erase or modify data of files; however, it was most certainly capable of doing this and therefore had enormous potential for primary damage. However, even its secondary damage was substantial; the secondary damage was caused by the efforts required to purge the worm from the system.

Due to the large number of sites affected (a very high percentage of all active participants in the network), this cost was estimated to have amounted to many man years of work, even though it was relatively easy to eliminate the worm by rebooting each system because the worm was never permanently stored.

One reason this worm made great waves was that it caused the first major infection of mainframe computers. Prior to this incident, various computer viruses (causing various degrees of damage; see Section 2.2.1) had been reported but only for personal computers. Since operating systems for these systems are typically less sophisticated and had originally been designed for personal use only, and not for networking, they had been considered more susceptible to computer virus attacks. Thus, threats to mainframes from viruses were thought to be less likely than similar threats to personal computers and workstations. The November 2, 1988, incident destroyed this myth in less than half a day, the time it took to shut down Internet and the computers affected by it.

While the November 2, 1988, incident involved a worm, the known personal computer infiltrations were caused by viruses. As noted, most of them affected floppy disks (probably because of their relatively simple internal format) and caused damage, in some cases rather substantial. Many computer viruses came from bulletin boards or 'free ware', but at least two (the rather harmless Freehand Virus and the damage-causing Amiga Virus) came from regularly distributed software.

2.3 Outlook

For years, computer viruses, worms and other threats were dismissed as exotic oddities. With rapidly increasing speed, this assessment has changed to the point where paranoia sets in. In spite of dire predictions to the contrary, the data processing community will adapt and learn how to live with the presence of viruses and the like (since detection of viruses is not feasible in general — see Chapters 6 and 7). In the process, some convenience may have to be sacrificed and some of the free-wheeling ways will have to be replaced by a more structured (i.e., restrictive) approach to producing and using software. This may simply be part of computing's coming of age — free love versus safe sex.

Overall, up until now the known virus and worm attacks have caused a good deal, but not a staggering amount of damage. However, as indicated in Section 3.6, all of the viruses and worms have had the ability to cause enormous damage; technically, all have had access to virtually all files of the infected systems and could have erased or modified them. While many did not do this, it is quite possible that someone modifies a 'harmless' virus to do just that.

There is speculation that new generations of computer viruses may appear that have greater flexibility and are more virulent. Since prophets have been known to be wrong, what follows is the author's current and very personal view. In my opinion, there will be no dramatically more threatening generations of computer viruses. This is primarily because current viruses already have all the functionality one would want if one were to destroy software and data. Virulence in a virus or worm is actually a disadvantage since it leads to early detection. A much greater danger is stealth, which is already practiced, or at least attempted, by current attackers. (In this context it is interesting to note that several viruses and worms were detected because they did not manage to act sufficiently stealthily.)

Thus the future will probably see more sophisticated viruses and worms, using more intimate knowledge of certain operating systems. However, it should be kept in mind that a virus tailored to one very specific system will have much less of an impact than one that can infect a large class of systems (e.g., any system running some version of Unix). On the other hand, general system flaws will probably be remedied rapidly, forcing the attacker to be more savvy. This is likely to increase the size of these complicated virus and worm programs, and this in turn will help in detecting them more rapidly as they will use up more space (see Chapter 7). Incidentally, this is the same reason why truly evolving viruses are unlikely to play a major role in the near future (see Section 3.3). Thus, in my opinion it is unlikely that the threat stemming from computer viruses and worms will increase dramatically due to new advances in virus and worm design.

2.4 Bibliographical Notes

The development of and experiences with the Xerox Palo Alto Research Center Worm programs are outlined in [31]. The series of articles on the game CoreWar appeared in the magazine *Scientific American* ([32] and [33], with [34] being a manual on how to conduct core wars). Reports on the Freehand, Lehigh, Brain, Hebrew University, Amiga, Flu-Shot 4, and IBM Christmas Tree viruses are contained in [35]. The first four of this list as well as the Scores Virus are described in [15]. The Scores Virus was reported in [14] as well. The first factual accounts of the November 2, 1988, attack, the first known successful attack involving mainframe computers, were provided in [4] and [10]; more details about it will be given in Chapter 4.

Chapter Three

Definitions

For any system under attack the most worrisome aspect of a virus or similar attacker is its ability to destroy data and software. However, from a technical point of view the most alarming aspect of the attackers under discussion in this book is their ability to self-replicate. In other words, the piece of software that performs the subversion has the ability of making copies of itself and transmitting them to other users in the computer or to other computer systems in the network. Obviously, each of these copies now can wreak havoc in turn, wherever it may be - and replicate itself as well. Thus, it may be sufficient to set one such program loose in one computer, in order to affect most or all computers and most or all users in a given network.

Since more and more computers are interconnected by networks, the threat of subversion assumes literally global dimensions. As we saw in the last chapter, in several cases (e.g., the Pakistani Virus), national boundaries are no hurdle for viruses. In fact, several major computer networks are quite international, involving most technologically advanced countries. Furthermore, a good deal of software is shared using these networks and other means, thereby increasing the potential for the transmission of viruses.

In order to get a more precise notion of the virus attacks that are of interest here, we must define a few important terms, including logical bombs and logical time bombs, computer viruses, and worms. It should be kept in mind however that this area of computer security is still quite young; consequently there continue to be disagreements among researchers about the precise delineation between certain terms.

3.1 Logical Bombs

A logical bomb is a piece of code, usually embedded in other software, that is only activated (i.e., executed) if a certain condition is met. Activation of an embedded logical bomb may abort a program run or erase data or program files. If the condition of execution is not satisfied at all times, it may be regarded as a logical time bomb. Logical bombs that are activated in every invocation are usually not as harmful as time bombs, since their actions can be observed in every execution of the affected software. A typical time bomb is one where a disgruntled employee inserts into complex software that is frequently executed (a compiler or a payroll system, for example) a code that will abort the execution of the software or do other damage, for instance after a certain date — naturally chosen to fall after the date of the employee's resignation or dismissal.

Note that some programming errors may appear to be time bombs; e.g., there is wide-spread suspicion that many programs that use dates will handle the transition from the year 1999 to the year 2000 in a less than graceful manner, since frequently only the last two digits of the year are stored, but in many cases numerical ordering is used, causing the year '00' to come before the year '99'. In general, however, virtually all intentional logical bombs are malicious. Typically, the author of a logical time bomb is a programmer in a trusted position who abuses this trust. Most frequently the motive is revenge for perceived injustice inflicted upon the programmer by his or her employer. While revenge by a logical time bomb can be highly disruptive, the damage is usually limited, both in time, as it is likely that the bomb will be detected and removed immediately after it has wreaked havoc for the first time (assuming it is recognized), and in its spread (since it does not replicate, it should not affect other sites).

Note that the extent of a malicious action is directly related to the probability of detecting it; in other words, if a logical time bomb shuts down all operations or erases all files, it will be noticed immediately; on the other hand, if it only changes a few characters in an obscure file, it may never be detected.

3.2 Trojan Horses

There are other terms related to logical bombs, most notably that of Trojan horse. The name Trojan Horse is derived from Greek mythology; as Homer relates in the Iliad, after an unsuccessful ten-year siege of the city of Troy, the Greeks in their efforts to defeat Troy and recover Helena resorted to a ruse. Pretending to end the war they lifted the siege, and embarked on their ships, leaving behind a large wooden horse, ostensibly as a present to the gods of the attacked city, but actually containing a select band of Greek warriors. The citizens of Troy accepted the presumed gift by pulling it inside the city walls, which allowed the hidden warriors to emerge under the cover of darkness and open the city gates for the returned Greek army, thereby sealing the fate of (Homer's) Troy.

Homer's tale provides a nice analogy to this type of program. Like the mythical Trojan horse, a Trojan horse program pretends to be a perfectly legitimate program, for example a compiler or a file handler, which has access to other users' files. This legitimate-purpose program is however subverted with the objective of violating security constraints. Examples of unauthorized actions are obtaining access to users' passwords or modifying records in protected files. The perpetrator could be a programmer who worked on the legitimate-purpose software and inserted a code that performs the action or it could be someone who circumvented the security of the legitimate-purpose trusted software to insert a malicious-purpose code. From this description it should be clear that a Trojan horse is basically just another form of logical bomb, except that the method of inserting it into software is somewhat different: usually, a logical bomb is explicitly inserted by a programmer, while a Trojan horse resorts to trickery to entice an unsuspecting user into running an alluring program that then inserts the logical bomb.

3.3 Computer Viruses

A computer virus is a logical time bomb that is able to replicate itself, to subvert a computer system in some way, and to transmit copies of itself to other hardware and/or software systems. Each of the copies in turn may self-replicate and affect yet other systems. A computer virus usually attaches itself to an existing program and is therefore permanently stored with this program. It follows that it is not sufficient to simply switch off the computer system in order to purge the virus; any use of an infected program stored on disk or tape will reintroduce the virus into the system. Moreover, it is not entirely obvious that using back-up tapes to retrieve old files will result in uninfected files - a file may have been infected long before the virus is active, and if one does not know how the virus looks and what to search for in a file (or if it is infeasible, in the case of very large system), one can not be certain that one's restored files are free of viruses. This is where the delay built into many viruses is crucial: a virus may seemingly lie dormant (in that no action can be noticed), yet it is present and can in fact infect other users.

The analogy with a biological virus should be obvious from the above, including the ability of lying dormant for some time. It should not be carried to extremes, however, as some authors have done. In particular it is pointless to discuss whether the name is appropriate from a biological point of view - there is no question that by now the term 'computer virus' or just 'virus' has irrevocably entered into the computer jargon.

One aspect that received quite a bit of theoretical attention but has not had much practical import is the notion of 'evolved' virus. This connotes the ability of the virus to evolve, i.e., change appearance and/or behavior, over time. There are (at least) two possible approaches. One consists of providing several branches in a program; this is rather unsophisticated and certainly covered by our definition of virus. Thus we do not consider this an evolved virus. The other one is much more interesting, and also at first glance much more alarming. It concerns programs that in response to outside stimuli change physical appearance (the statements they are comprised of) and behavior (the actions they take).

Let us determine the likely threat stemming from an evolved virus. Since every program is fundamentally deterministic, it must be external factors that cause a program to evolve. In other words, it must be the environment in which the virus is inserted which is the unknown factor, since the virus program itself is initially given. This implies that the virus must have some type of learning capability. While in theory it is possible to write programs that adapt to a given environment and learn from it, thereby evolving, in practice such programs tend to be very long and would draw undesired attention by using extensive resources (space for storing, cpu time for execution, transmission time for sending), possibly significantly more than the infected program itself would be expected to consume. Furthermore, such programs require a thorough background in artificial intelligence or a similar discipline; this clearly reduces the number of possible perpetrators (but not to zero!). Thus, we conclude that the perceived threat from the evolved virus is overrated, since they are quite unlikely to occur in practise. This is also confirmed by experience; none of the viruses that were ever observed had the ability to evolve.

3.4 Computer Worms

A worm is another member of our bestiary. It is very similar to a computer virus in that it is self-replicating and subverts a system; however, it is usually a self-contained program that enters a system via regular communication channels in a network and then generates its own commands. Therefore it is frequently not permanently stored as (part of) a file but rather exists only in the main memory of the computer. This means in particular that ordinarily the powering down of the computer system will purge the worm. Note however that this does not preclude subsequent reinfection when the computer is operational again. This is particularly unpleasant in the case of a large network where there is the danger of reinfection as long as any one infected site is operational.

Note that a logical bomb resident in a piece of software that is explicitly copied to another system by the user may appear as a virus to the users, even though it is not, since it is neither self-replicating nor auto-relocatable. For a comparison of these terms, see Figure 4.

	Delayed action	Self-repli-cation	Auto-relo-cation	Permanently stored as part of a legitimate file
Logical bomb	No	No	No	Yes
Logical time bomb	Yes	No	No	Yes
Trojan horse	No	No	No	Yes
Virus	Likely	Yes	Yes	Yes
Worm	Likely	Yes	Yes	No

Figure 4. Comparison of various attackers

3.5 The Process of Viral Infection

The process of viral infection is similar to that of inserting a Trojan horse, except that a virus can of course replicate itself. In most cases, the insertion of the virus is originally by tricking (exceptions are the Freehand and Amiga viruses; see Section 2.2.1) the user into running a program that infects other software. This process is as follows.

(a) The perpetrator creates and makes available an alluring program V which contains the virus.

(b) The victim executes the program V.

(c) The program V copies the virus (portion of V that constitutes the virus) to other software under the victim's control (software to which he has write or modify access). This is typically done without the victim noticing it immediately.

(d) All software under the victim's control now contains the virus and can in turn infect other software when executed.

3.6 Types of Damage

Each of the three types of subversion mechanisms, logical bombs, viruses, and worms, can, but need not, cause damage. We have already discussed instances where bombs and viruses merely printed out some rather innocuous message on the screen and then erased themselves, without destroying data or causing other disruptions. These can be considered as relatively harmless pranks, an exhibitionistic display of programming prowess.

However, it should be clearly understood that these subversion mechanisms, especially the self-replicating ones, have enormous potential for damage. This may be due to deliberate and explicit erasure or modification of data and software; we will call these *primary action* or *primary damage*. It may also be due to far less obvious *secondary effects.* These are typically unintended by the perpetrator, due either to ignorance or carelessness. However, some secondary effects are clearly quite deliberate and with malicious intent.

3.6.1 Primary Damage

The most spectacular damage is usually the whole-sale destruction of data and software. This may be by erasing floppy disks or hard disks. Such actions are invariably detected with very little delay, thereby effectively preventing indirect consequential damages. Much more insidious damage can be wrought by subtle changes in files. To understand this better, consider a scenario of industrial sabotage where a virus alters the parameters of an industrial control program. These changes could be made such that the yield of some process is decreased over time (the virus can periodically change the parameters), yet it is unlikely that such a phenomenon would be blamed on a "faulty" (i.e., infected) computer program.

3.6.2 Secondary Damage

We pointed out in Section 2.1 how it was very early on discovered that self-replicating auto-relocatable programs can be very difficult to control, especially if something went wrong with them. As our brief history of attacks shows, on more than one occasion a virus was detected before it could do primary damage, since its unchecked self-replication revealed its presence. The Hebrew University Virus is one example.

In a similar vein, the November 2, 1988, incident indicated very drastically the secondary damages that can occur. This worm arrived via electronic mail; arrival of mail activates a process that handles the receiving of mail. Typically, in order to avoid mail back logs, this process has high priority, i.e., if there are any other processes executing they will be suspended until the mail handler is finished. Thus, if the system receives many mail messages, a user may get the impression that the system is greatly slowed down. If these mail messages are all copies of the same worm, which keeps on replicating and mailing copies to other sites, regardless of whether they had been infected previously or not, it is clear that the system can easily be saturated. This causes damage even though no data or software are ever erased. Another secondary effect can be caused by the infiltrator if it uses excessive amounts of disk space (in the case of a virus) or memory (in the case of a worm). For instance a virus that replicates unrestrictedly, reinfecting already infected sites, may cause the system to request more disk space than is available, thereby possibly causing the system to crash.

A more direct type of secondary damage occurs when a virus or similar attacker infects computer systems, not with the purpose of destroying data or disrupting operations, but with the intent of using the access thus obtained to users' files to search for specific types of information which, when encountered, can be sent back to the perpetrator. This then amounts to espionage, either military or industrial. It is not difficult to imagine an infected military database system which is surreptitiously used to examine files for certain key words, such as SDI or

Strategic Defense Initiative, and then mails copies of all files containing the keywords to some far-away spy. Similarly, in an industrial setting, an infected compiler could well be subverted so as to mail copies of programs containing certain trade secrets to a competitor.

3.6.3 Harmless or Vicious?

Many viruses and worms (but not all!) that have been encountered in the past few years were relatively harmless pranks whose main purpose appears the demonstration of how clever the programmer was who wrote the virus or worm program. This includes for instance the November 2, 1988, incident, and several PC viruses. However, it should be noted that any harmless attacker, once isolated, can be easily modified into a truly malicious threat to software and data (see Section 4.2). This can be done without any special knowledge; so even persons who would never be able to write a virus or worm program themselves can pose a substantial threat to computer installations. Thus, one should never underestimate the damages that even a supposedly harmless virus or worm can ultimately cause.

3.7 Bibliographical Notes

Most of the bestiary presented in this chapter is defined in [1], [2], and [3]. Worms specifically appear in [31]. The papers [36] and [37] contain extensive discussions about terminology, the differentiation between terms, and the appropriateness of calling a computer virus a virus. In fact, it has even been suggested (in [3]) that the Darwinian theory of Survial of the Fittest may provide a simile for a computer system where there are "general purpose evolutionary mechanisms ... used for the generation of both viruses and viral detection ... systems", a highly speculative and very far-fetched notion that will certainly not occur very soon, if ever.

Chapter Four

Examples

In this chapter we provide necessary information about the operation of viruses and worms and examine a few incidents in more detail. We also give a generic example of a virus.

4.1 Ken Thompson's Trojan C Compiler

In his lecture on the occasion of being awarded the 1983 Turing Award of the Association for Computing Machinery, Ken Thompson outlines the development of a compiler that permits him to circumvent the usual constraints on access to files. It does this as follows. The binary code of the C compiler is modified causing the login command to be 'miscompiled' so that it accepts both the intended password (P) and a particular other password (P') to be used for surreptitious access to any file supposedly protected by password P. Thompson describes a method that achieves this without leaving any trace in any source code. This enable hin to log in to any computer account, provided his C compiler was used.

4.2 A Virus Template

Below follows a template for a virus, formulated in pseudo-Pascal. It omits all details; instead the comments indicate the tasks to be performed. It should be clear that certain operations required in the template are quite target dependent; for example, the procedure GET_EXECUTABLE _FILE will depend heavily on the file defintion scheme implemented in the target system. This is a major reason why most viruses attack only one type of computers or operating systems. We also note that in practice the virus will have to be written in a language that is in conformity with the program that is to be infected. Thus, it will usually be in machine-executable or object code rather than in a higher level language. This also helps in avoiding detection as most programmers will never inspect object code, only source code. Here then is the template:

```
procedure INFECT_PROGRAM;

var INFECTED: boolean;
    EXECUTABLE_NAME: FILE_NAME_STRING;

    procedure GET_EXECUTABLE_FILE(var EXECUTABLE_NAME:
                 FILE_NAME_STRING);
    begin
      { get list of executable files according to file system
        definition; randomly select one file of this list and
        return }
    end;

    function ALREADY_INFECTED(EXECUTABLE_NAME: FILE_NAME_STRING)
               : boolean;
    begin
      { check a specific address in the file to see whether it is
        identical to that of the virus program; if so return true
        else return false  }
    end;

    procedure DUPLICATE_AND_PREPEND(EXECUTABLE_NAME:
                 FILE_NAME_STRING);
    begin
      { prepend word for word the procedures INFECT_PROGRAM,
        INFECT_CONDITION, and VIRUS_BODY to the file with name
        EXECUTABLE_NAME                                          }
    end;

begin
  INFECTED := false;
  while not INFECTED do
    begin
      GET_EXECUTABLE_FILE(EXECUTABLE_NAME);
      if not ALREADY_INFECTED(EXECUTABLE_NAME) then
        begin
          DUPLICATE_AND_PREPEND(EXECUTABLE_NAME);
          INFECTED := true
        end
    end
end;

function INFECT_CONDITION : boolean;
begin
  { a triggering condition for infection is tested for;
    if the condition is satisfied, return true else return false}
end;

procedure VIRUS_BODY;
begin
  if INFECT_CONDITION then INFECT_PROGRAM
end;
```

Clearly the function ALREADY_INFECTED is not necessary for the correct operation of the virus; it merely ensures that a program is only infected once. While in principle this contributes little to the virus, in practice the ability to avoid reinfection of an already infected program is important to avoid detection of the virus's presence. A similar comment is in order about the function INFECT_ CONDITION; it allows to delay infections. For example, in order to make the virus more unobtrusive, the condition might ensure that only every fifth program is infected. This may be desirable if the virus is relatively large and therefore uses up a good deal of storage.

Noticeably absent from this template is any action that would cause primary damage. However, it is fairly easy to add the requisite procedures (cf Section 3.6.3). Here they are:

```
procedure VIRAL_ACTION;
  begin
    { whatever action }
  end;

function ACTION_CONDITION : boolean;
  begin
    { a triggering condition for viral action is tested for;
      if the condition is satisfied return true else return
      false}
  end;
```

Additionally, we now must replace the procedure VIRUS_BODY in the above template by the following:

```
procedure VIRUS_BODY;
  begin
    if INFECT_CONDITION then INFECT_PROGRAM;
    if ACTION_CONDITION then VIRAL_ACTION
  end;
```

Just as in the case of the function INFECT_ CONDITION, the boolean function ACTION_CONDITION is designed to delay action in order to make it more difficult to detect the presence of the virus.

4.3 Viral Actions

In order to get a better appreciation of the malicious actions a virus can perform we will take a closer look at a particular operating system. We choose the operating systems PC-DOS and MS-DOS for personal computers and describe the format of a 360K floppy disk, the most commonly used type of diskette for these operating systems. Each floppy disk has on each side 40 tracks, each of which contains nine sectors of 512 bytes. Thus, the two-sided disk has a total storage capacity of 2x40x9x512 or 368,640 bytes. Of the 720 sectors, the first twelve, numbered 0 through 11, contain the vital dictionary information without which the disk can not be used. Specifically:

Sector 0: this sector contains the disk parameter table (DPT); it contains information such as the number of sides formatted, the number of tracks, the number of sectors per track, and the number of bytes per sector.

Sectors 1 and 2: the File Allocation Table (FAT) is stored here. It shows where each file is located; if a file is broken up into several portions, the FAT indicates which sectors in which order store the file. Note that these sectors need not be contiguous. The FAT also indicates the free sectors on the disk.

Sectors 3 and 4: these two sectors contain a copy of the information in Sectors 1 and 2.

Sectors 5 through 11: these sectors store name, size, date and time of creation and other attributes about each file.

On ordinary disks, the remaining sectors (numbered 12 through 719) contain data and programs. An exception are the disks with systems programs required to make the disk bootable. In these disks, 32 sectors starting with Sector 12 contain IBMBIO.COM or MSBIO.COM (IBMBIO.SYS or MSBIO.SYS for later versions of the operating systems), followed by IBMDOS.COM or MSDOS.COM (IBMDOS.SYS or MSDOS.SYS) on 56 sectors starting in Sector 44; finally, COMMAND.COM starts in Sector 160 and occupies 48 sectors.

From this description it is apparent that the 360K disk has a very rigid format. In ordinary disks, the first twelve sectors contain vital disk data, in a bootable disk the first 208 sectors contain the vital disk data as well as the disk's operating system. Similar statements hold for other types of floppy disks and also for hard disks, although the structure for hard disks is more complex. In every case, however, the vital data are stored in a fixed location on the disk.

Here is a list of possible viral actions, each causing primary damage.

(A) A virus may destroy the file allocation table (FAT) of a floppy disk. This renders the disk unreadable and effectively destroys all information on it. (While products exist that allow one to read sectors without access to the FAT, it may be impossible to piece together longer files which are stored in non-contiguous locations.)

(B) A virus may change disk assignments resulting in files being written to the wrong disk. One way in which this can erase a file is by directing it to RAM (random access memory) instead of floppy or hard disk; since this change would not be known to the programmer, he or she expects the file to be permanently saved on disk, when in fact it evaporates as soon as the system is switched off, since RAM stores information only when it is under power.

(C) A virus may erase specific executable programs or data files, either explicitly or by tampering with the FAT portion that pertains to that file.

(D) A virus may selectively alter data in files.

(E) A virus may format specific tracks of a disk or even the entire disk. This effectively erases all information in the affected sectors.

Additional viral actions that are damaging but do not cause primary damage are the following.

(F) A virus may suppress the execution of programs resident in RAM.

(G) A virus may reduce the amount of free space available on disk. This is an obvious consequence of making a copy of the virus that is stored on disk. By itself, this action should not interfere with the working of programs.

(H) A virus may cause the system to crash or to 'hang' so that it does not respond any longer to any keystrokes and requires a cold boot.

4.4 The Internet Attack

As repeatedly mentioned before, in the evening of November 2, 1988, an attacker began to bring to its knees a large portion of the Internet, a collection of networks consisting of approximately 60,000 computers, interconnected via the network protocol TCP/IP. It was estimated that about 10 percent of these, or 6,000 computers, succumbed to the attack. In this section we take a closer look at the attacker, outline how it subverted its victims, who they were and what characteristics they had, and also what the attacker did not do. We discuss the flaws in the attacker which enabled users to detect its presence and the steps that were taken to determine how it works. Since the attacker was a worm according to our definition (see Chapter 3), we will call it the Internet Worm.

Note: This section is somewhat more technical than the other sections. A certain familiarity with UNIX is assumed. Readers not interested in the technical details of this attack may skim this section or omit it completely.

4.4.1 Victims and their Characteristics

There were only two types of computers that were attacked successfully, namely SUN Work Stations and VAX computers. All systems that were subverted ran the operating system Berkeley Standard Distribution UNIX (BSD UNIX) or systems derived from it.

Once resident in a computer, the worm attempted to subvert other machines on the network. The methods it used to do this were sendmail in debug mode, remote execution using the commands rexec and rsh, and finger (only for VAXes). It attacked accounts with obvious passwords, including those with no password, and accounts where the password was the user name, the user name repeated twice, the 'nick name' (a feature that allows users to have aliases which are stored in the system), or the last name of the user, spelled either forward or backward. It also subverted accounts whose passwords were included in a dictionary with 432 words (which was contained in the code of the worm), accounts with passwords in the file /usr/dict/words (a UNIX system file), and accounts which trusted other machines via the .rhosts mechanism. The methods are explained in more detail below.

- **sendmail:** this mail system has a debug mode which contains two features whose combination was successfully exploited by the worm. The first feature is the ability to send a mail message with the sendmail program itself as recipient of the message. Thus, the program will execute with input which comes from the body of the message. The second feature is that in some cases a specific program is executed when mail is received. This occurs normally for aliasing, forwarding of mail, vacation notification (the intended recipient replies that he is on vacation until a certain date), and personal mail processing systems, such as sorters. Normally, the execution of a program is not allowed for incoming connections. The Internet Worm exploited these two features by giving as 'recipient' a command to strip off the mail header and transfer the headerless message to a command interpreter. The body was a script which caused the remainder of the modules of the Internet Worm to be transferred from the host that originated the exchange to the target host; it also generated the commands to link and execute these modules. Object code for both VAX and SUN was transferred, thereby enabling the worm to infect either type of computer. Although this attack did not work if the debug mode of sendmail was not enabled, the worm was aided by the fact that in both 4.2 and 4.3 BSD UNIX releases, the debug mode was enabled by default.

- **rexec:** the Berkeley remote execution protocol requires the user name and the password to be sent over the net in plaintext. This was exploited by the worm; it used only those (name,password)-pairs that had already been found valid at the current host. This local validation was greatly facilitated by the existence of a world-readable file (/etc/passw) that contains, for every user on the system, the user name and the corresponding encrypted password. Such a file can be downloaded and, using the dictionary attack, easy passwords can be decrypted.

The dictionary attack is based on a file of common words which programmers are likely to use. As explained in Section 1.2, people tend to use simple passwords because they can remember them better. Alternatively, complicated (i.e., difficult to remember) passwords are often recorded somewhere, possibly even in a computer file which may be in plaintext (not encrypted) and protected only by an easy-to-remember password. (The bad habit of creating files of passwords was exploited by the attacker reported on in Chapter 5.)

In the dictionary attack, an encrypted password is decrypted as follows (see Fig. 5). Each of the words in the dictionary file is encrypted; if the result of the encryption of word w matches the encrypted password, then w is for all practical purposes the plaintext (unencrypted) password that will give access to a file or an account. In the case of the Internet worm, part of the code itself contained a dictionary file of 432 words; since the worm had to perform all operations without the benefit of permanent storage, it had to bring its own dictionary file with it. This dictionary file is given in Figure 6. (The contents of this file are sufficiently eclectic that one might surmise that it was formed by observing/intercepting actual passwords. From this point of view, it is interesting to note that there were 11 words of length 3 and 27 of length 4; in other words, almost 9% of all words were so short that a most simple-minded systematic enumeration would catch them easily.) While this file is very short, it should be kept in mind that in other types of attack (see Chapter 5), encrypted passwords can be downloaded to other computers and can be attacked with arbitrarily complex dictionary files. The only requirement for this attack is that the encryption function be known, and this is usually met.

- **rsh:** this is the Berkeley remote shell program; it is

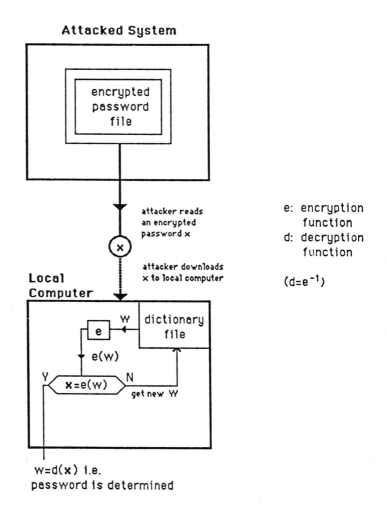

Figure 5. The Dictionary Attack

aaa	carmen	engineer	herbert	minimum	rainbow	super
academia	carolina	enterprise	hiawatha	minsky	raindrop	superstage
aerobics	caroline	enzyme	hibernia	moguls	raleigh	support
airplane	cascades	ersatz	honey	moose	random	supported
albany	castle	establish	horse	morley	rascal	surfer
albatross	cat	estate	horus	mozart	really	suzanne
albert	cayuga	euclid	hutchins	nancy	rebecca	swearer
alex	celtics	evelyn	imbroglio	napoleon	remote	symmetry
alexander	cerulean	extension	imperial	nepenthe	rick	tangerine
algebra	change	fairway	include	ness	ripple	tape
aliases	charles	felicia	ingres	network	robotics	target
alphabet	charming	fender	inna	newton	rochester	tarragon
ama	charon	fermat	innocuous	next	rolex	taylor
amorphous	chester	fidelity	irishman	noxious	romano	telephone
analog	cigar	finite	isis	nutrition	ronald	temptation
anchor	classic	fishers	japan	nyquist	rosebud	thailand
andromache	clusters	flakes	jessica	oceanography	rosemary	tiger
animals	coffee	float	jester	ocelot	roses	toggle
answer	coke	flower	jixian	olivetti	ruben	tomato
anthropogenic	collins	flowers	johnny	olivia	rules	topography
anvils	commrades	foolproof	joseph	oracle	ruth	tortoise
anything	computer	football	joshua	orca	sal	toyota
aria	condo	foresight	judith	orwell	saxon	trails
ariadne	cookie	format	juggle	osiris	scamper	trivial
arrow	cooper	forsythe	julia	outlaw	scheme	trombone
arthur	cornelius	fourier	kathleen	oxford	scott	tubas
athena	couscous	fred	kermit	pacific	scotty	tuttle
atmosphere	creation	friend	kernel	painless	secret	umesh
aztecs	creosote	frighten	kirkland	pakistan	sensor	unhappy
azure	cretin	fun	knight	pam	serenity	unicorn
bacchus	daemon	fungible	ladle	papers	sharks	unknown

bailey	dancer	gabriel	lambda	password	sharon	urchin
banana	daniel	gardner	lamination	patricia	sheffield	utility
bananas	danny	garfield	larkin	penguin	sheldon	vasant
bandit	dave	gauss	larry	peoria	shiva	vertigo
banks	december	george	lazarus	percolate	shivers	vicky
barber	defoe	gertrude	lebesque	persimmon	shuttle	village
baritone	deluge	ginger	lee	persona	signature	virginia
bass	desperate	glacier	leland	pete	simon	warren
bassoon	develop	gnu	leroy	peter	simple	water
batman	dieter	golfer	lewis	philip	singer	weenie
beater	digital	gorgeous	light	phoenix	single	whatnot
beauty	discovery	gorges	lisa	pierre	smile	whiting
beethoven	disney	gosling	louis	pizza	smiles	whitney
beloved	dog	gouge	lynne	plover	smooch	will
benz	drought	graham	macintosh	plymouth	smother	william
beowulf	duncan	gryphon	mack	polynomial	snatch	williamsburg
berkeley	eager	guest	maggot	pondering	snoopy	willie
berliner	easier	guitar	magic	pork	soap	winston
beryl	edges	gumption	malcolm	poster	socrates	wisconsin
beverly	edinburgh	guntis	mark	praise	sossina	wizard
bicameral	edwin	hacker	markus	precious	sparrows	wombat
bob	edwina	hamlet	marty	prelude	spit	woodwind
brenda	egghead	handily	marvin	prince	spring	wormwood
brian	eiderdown	happening	master	princeton	springer	yacov
bridget	eileen	harmony	maurice	protect	squires	yang
broadway	einstein	harold	mellon	protozoa	strangle	yellowstone
bumbling	elephant	harvey	merlin	pumpkin	stratford	yosemite
burgess	elizabeth	hebrides	mets	puneet	stuttgart	zap
campanile	ellen	heinlein	michael	puppet	subway	zimmerman
cantor	emerald	hello	michelle	rabbit	success	
cardinal	engine	help	mike	rachmaninoff	summer	

Figure 6. The Internet Virus Dictionary File

basically a remote execution system. For convenience, a file (/etc/hosts.equiv) can contain a list of hosts trusted by the host where this file resides. The remote host can pass the user name from a trusted port to a recipient and the target host will accept this as proof that the connection is legitimate. The worm took advantage of a design flaw in this system, namely that the receiving host knows the remote host only by its network address which can be forged.

- **finger:** the finger daemon (fingerd) contains a buffer that is allocated on a stack. Because in entering items on the stack, no range checking is performed, the worm created an overflow condition in the buffer; this allowed the creation of a bogus stack frame which caused the code to be executed upon return. This code could then be used for subversive purposes. This attack succeeded only on 4.3 BSD VAX systems; it was not written for SUNs and did not work for Ultrix on VAXes since Ultrix does not include a finger daemon.

4.4.2 What the Worm Did Not Do

While the Internet Worm caused substantial secondary damage by clogging the network to the point that some victimized systems were unable to carry out useful work, it did not destroy or attempt to destroy any data of programs, it did not insert (logical) time bombs into any programs, and it did not gain privileged access (system privileges). However, it must be noted that this could only be ascertained once the complete code of the worm was known. To get this knowledge required an enormous amount of effort on the part of several teams (see Section 4.4.5 below).

4.4.3 Flaws

The major flaw of the worm design was in the test that was supposed to prevent reinfection of already infected systems. Because of timing flaws, which to a large degree were fundamentally problems that had to do with several worms arriving at a node at the same time, the worm was detected since multiple infections increased the load on many subverted machines which in turn drew attention to the worm's existence and eventually caused its purge from the Internet. Had these flaws been absent, it is conceivable that the worm would have existed practically forever and unnoticed by anybody.

4.4.4 Defenses of the Worm

In an effort to evade detection the worm covered its tracks and camouflaged itself. Techniques of erasing indicators of its presence included the following:
- It erased its arguments after they had been processed. This prevented the process status command from revealing how it was invoked.
- It deleted the executing binary code from memory; thus the data were intact but without logical address and could only be referenced by the execution of the program. Consequently, the program vanished after exiting. To capture the file, it was necessary to reboot the system while the worm was executing, in which case the file salvager recovers it after the reboot.
- It prevented core dumps that might give it away, which could be caused by any errors or incompatibilities in the program.

As for camouflage, the worm used several schemes:
- It compiled under the name of the Bourne Shell (sh), a commonly used command interpreter, thereby avoiding detection.
- It effectively reset its resource utilization to zero, by splitting into a parent and a child, approximately every three minutes. The parent exited, leaving the child in the same place as a new process.
- It hid constants in its program by exclusive-oring them with the hexadecimal number 81 (201 in octal, or 129 in decimal).

4.4.5 Attempts at Defending Against the Worm

There were several approaches that computer installations implemented in their (initially rather desperate) attempts to protect themselves and their customers against the worm. It should be noted that it was by no means clear at the beginning that the worm did not cause any primary damage. This uncertainty created a large measure of urgency on the part of the programming teams that formed to combat the worm. Some of the approaches were initial and rather global in scope, such as full isolation from the network and switching off the mail service (both were easy to do and very effective, but inconvenienced users). Others were later reactions based on some partial knowledge about the inner workings of the worm; here we mention disabling the debug mode in sendmail (easy to do and no inconvenience to users), disabling or fixing the finger daemon (easy to do and hardly or no inconvenience), and requiring users with weak passwords to use new ones (a rather major change, but one that only inconvenienced users who indirectly aided the worm in subverting the systems). These three schemes were only effective if they were done in combination; one alone would at best slow the worm down, but did not prevent infections. Another very effective, albeit somewhat drastic, measure was to rename the UNIX C compiler and linker (cc and ld).

In trying to find out what actions to take in order to defend their systems against the worm, many systems programmer teams attempted to find out as much as possible about the worm. The ultimate objective was to obtain a source code version of the entire worm program. Since the worm existed only in binary form in the systems, it was necessary to 'decompile' it, i.e., derive a higher-level language version that compiles into the given executable code. Once this was accomplished, it was possible to analyze the strategies that it used; it was also possible to devise methods of purging the worm from the systems.

4.5 Bibliographical Notes

The insidious C compiler for subverting the login command in Unix (and other C-based systems) was described by Thompson in [38]. The virus template is an adaptation of the one given by Cohen in [2]. The description of the 360K disk is taken from [35]; this paper also contains a list of viral actions. The Internet attack is described in extensive detail in [37]; most of Section 4.4 is taken from it. [39] also provides a good deal of technical information about the Internet Worm. [40] discusses techniques of cracking passwords. In [41], some conclusions are drawn from the Internet attack with regard to setting and enforcing policies and procedures for managing large computer networks. The paper [42] discusses in detail a particular attack by a virus on a PC based system.

Chapter Five

Related Attacks

5.1 Types of Attacks

In terms of integrity violations the attacks we have discussed so far can be classified as follows:

- *Attacks by Trojan horse.* These are characterized by the initial subversion of software that is trusted by many users and has legitimate access to other files. It is important to realize that once the initial infiltration of the trusted software is completed, no violations of access privileges are required for the virus to spread arbitrarily. For example a compiler legitimately reads and writes files; thus the insertion of a copy of a virus into an executable or object file is legitimate as far as the access controls imposed on the compiler's actions are concerned. The only illegitimate action in this scenario is the insertion of the virus code into the compiler. The subsequent spreading of the virus can then quite possibly be carried out along perfectly legal channels and in ways that do not violate any access or flow controls of a given system. In particular, this implies that once a trusted piece of software is subverted, it is not sufficient to watch out for violations of access or flow controls in order to detect a virus before it does damage.

- *Attacks whereby the attacker obtains access to restricted software by circumventing access or flow controls.* This is typically done by guessing passwords or exploiting subtle flaws (including short-cuts) in the access or flow control mechanisms. Here there are certain techniques that one might use in order to recognize attacks and guard against them.

Guessing passwords implies that several passwords will be tried before one works. It is possible to disable access altogether to a domain after several passwords have been tried without success. While this method can be abused by pranksters intent on disrupting operations by disabling as many accounts as possible, it does provide some protection against intruders who systematically attempt to guess passwords. Additionally, it is possible to disable access paths or entry points to a system if many attempts of this nature have been observed to come through them.

Exploiting certain system flaws was one method that was used in the Internet attack. In principle, one might want to argue that such attacks are easily preventable; as soon as a flaw is discovered, it must be removed. However, this is by no means as easy as it appears.

Many operating systems, for example, have a multitude of known 'bugs'; their removal would often be prohibitively costly, and since they are known and affect only very few users very rarely (so the standard argument goes), they are not fixed, but at best documented. Thus, the question of decreasing the likelihood of a successful attack that exploits a flaw depends on the price one is willing to pay for removing the flaw. Since until recently viruses and similar attackers were considered merely exotic oddities but not real threats, most software vendors and/or computing centers preferred a risk that was considered practically zero over the definite, and sometimes predictably high, cost of reprogramming portions of their systems. This attitude is likely to change somewhat with the realization that the risk stemming from virus attacks is not as insignificant as was previously assumed and has in fact a potentially very high cost.

Another problem with the immediate elimination of flaws upon detection is that sometimes they may be convenient short-cuts whose elimination might be opposed by their users. Here, we come up against the question of trading convenience against security, which in theory is easy to resolve in favor of increased security, but in practice tends to go the other way.

5.2 The LBL Investigation

It should be noted that the above considerations apply equally to human attackers of computer systems. While in this scenario, the features of self-replication and auto relocation are absent, one deals here with human intelligence which can be far more difficult to control. For example, once a virus or similar attacker is located, careful examination of the code can usually delineate quite precisely how the attack is carried out and what the possible damage might be. This would even apply to an evolved virus, if the environment in which it occurs is known. In contrast to a fundamentally static, i.e., deterministic, program, this is not possible with human attackers, since they can change their behavior at will. This contention is illustrated by the following case study.

From August 1986 until almost one year later, the computer installations at Lawrence Berkeley Laboratory (LBL) in California were under attack. LBL is a U.S. government research institute that does not carry out any classified research. Its computer systems are interconnected by local area networks (LANs). LBL's LANs are connected nationally and internationally to a large number of other systems, military and defense contractors as well as universities and research organizations. Over the course of ten months, researchers at LBL, who apparently were the first to detect the intruder since it used LBL's facilities as hub for attempts to subvert others, observed the attack of about 450 computer systems; over 30 of them were successfully penetrated. Networks used by the intruder included Arpanet, Milnet, Tymnet, Internet, the Magnetic Fusion Energy network, and the High Energy Physics network.

Ironically, the first hint of a problem at LBL was provided by an accounting problem - a new account had been created without a corresponding billing address. Over the next few months, monitors and alarms were installed that allowed LBL personnel to watch the intruder's activities without letting him know that he was being watched. In many cases, LBL personnel notified sites under attack of the attempts causing those sites to block or remove the avenues the attacker used. As a consequence the attacker got the impression that most sites except LBL detected his presence while in reality practically no site except LBL detected him. Eventually, the intruder was traced to sources in West Germany. Later criminal investigations revealed that several persons were involved (see Section 5.3).

The intruder used a variety of techniques, none new, to enter computers and acquire system privileges.

- He tried to log in using common account names, such as root, guest, system, and field.
- He found valid account names by querying systems for currently logged in accounts, using the system functions who and finger.
- He tried default and common passwords.

In about five percent of the machines attacked, these very primitive techniques proved successful.

- Once logged in, he exploited certain system flaws to acquire system manager status.

An example of such a flaw is provided by the Gnu-Emacs text editor which includes its own mail system enabling users to send files to other users. To do this, it employs the Unix Set-User-Id-to-Root feature which lets part of the program execute with system manager privileges. It does not have any restriction as to where the file to be sent is moved; in particular, it does not prevent users from moving files into the system area. (Ordinarily, this would of course be a programming error which should be detected by the run time support system.) By creating a Unix shell that masqueraded as a utility program and moving it into the system area, the intruder tricked the system into executing his program under its (the system's) level of authority; the program was designed to grant the perpetrator system privileges.

- He scanned for plaintext (unencrypted) passwords to other systems. Since users frequently create files of passwords (a bad habit, but very common and virtually encouraged by difficult-to-remember passwords), this can be devastatingly effective.
- He derived passwords and access mechanisms from electronic mail messages, which frequently prepend the message with (some of) this information.
- He decrypted encrypted passwords.

In Unix and some other systems, passwords are stored in encrypted, but publicly readable form. Since the encryption method is known (it is just the password that is not known), it is easy to verify whether a certain plaintext password corresponds to a given ciphertext password retrieved from the encrypted password file. Using a dictionary, one can systematically decrypt all 'easy' passwords (i.e., all those passwords that correspond to words in the dictionary). This can clearly be done remotely by downloading the encrypted password file (see 4.4.1).

While these techniques were used by a human attacker, there is nothing that would prevent a clever programmer to incorporate any or all of them into a virus program. Indeed, some of them have been incorporated into existing attackers; for example, the dictionary attack was used by the Internet Worm. Therefore, all these techniques should be considered possible candidates for techniques that render viruses even more dangerous.

5.3 Bibliographical Notes

The attack at Lawrence Berkeley Laboratory is described in detail in [43]. The author also draws some conclusion about the vulnerability of systems as well as possible ways of combatting attacks. [44] and [45] reflect the aftermath of the investigation resulting from the LBL attack; five persons were reportedly arrested in Hanover, Hamburg, and West Berlin, accused of having illegally obtained access to military computer systems. This access allowed the group to obtain information which was allegedly sold to the K. G. B., the intelligence agency of the USSR. In [46] it was reported that one of the persons implicated and under criminal investigation in the spy scandal was found dead; as cause of death police reports suggest that K. Koch committed suicide by dousing himself with gasoline and setting himself on fire. In the absence of any witnesses, the K. G. B. connection and the method employed make this apparent suicide highly suspect.

PART III

DIAGNOSIS

Part III discusses theoretical and
practical aspects of how one can
determine that one's system is
infected by a virus or a worm.

Chapter Six

Detection of Viruses: Theoretical Aspects

In this chapter, we discuss the theoretical limits of detection. In particular, we show that it is impossible to detect whether a program contains a virus and discuss the implications of this result. We postpone the discussion of practical considerations until the next chapter.

6.1 Detection is Undecidable

We first show that, in a very strong sense, it is impossible to determine whether a given program is a virus. This then yields immediately the result that it is impossible to determine whether a given program contains a virus. Thus, in mathematical terms, detection of viruses is an undecidable problem. Since the proof is rather simple, we will present it before we outline the very practical implications of this seemingly very theoretical result.

Consider an algorithm A which for any given program P is able to decide whether or not P is a virus. Intuitively, such an algorithm is very appealing since it embodies precisely the notion of testing whether a program is a threat. However, we will show that such an algorithm is impossible; in other words, we will give a proof that such an algorithm cannot exist. Note that this is a much stronger statement than one that states that nobody has found such an algorithm yet; it means that there will never be such an algorithm no matter how much time, effort and ingenuity are invested in finding one.

Our proof will be indirect; we assume that such an algorithm A exists. By assumption, the algorithm A must work for any given program P. Now let V be a virus and consider the following program P*. Note that even though it appears that there is some circularity involved in this program, since P* occurs in its formulation, this is by no means the case: When A(P*) is called (at runtime), all arguments are known, thus this call will return an answer that is valid.

> P* : IF A(P*) returns false THEN V
>   ELSE do nothing.

In other words, if the algorithm A determines that P* is not a virus then the virus program V is invoked, making P* a virus; if on the other hand A(P*) were to return true then P* will do nothing, thereby making P* not a virus. In both cases, there is a contradiction which clearly shows that something is wrong. This something is the assumption that there exists an algorithm A that is able to determine for any given program, and therefore in particular for the program P*, whether or not it is a virus.

6.2 Implications

This method of showing that something cannot exist is a very simple instance of a general method called diagonalization; it is used to derive an internal contradiction which renders the original assumption absurd. We reiterate that this does not mean that even though so far nobody has been able to find an algorithm for determining viruses, eventually one might; rather it means that this problem falls into the same category as that of squaring the circle - there provably is no way of doing it.

While we now have the result that no general algorithm can exist that would allow one to decide for an arbitrary program whether or not it is a virus, this does not mean that it is never possible to determine for any program whether it is a virus; in fact, for most programs it is definitely possible to do this, but there is no general method that will always give an answer. Thus this problem is very similar to that of determining for two given context free grammars whether they generate the same language. This problem is of considerable practical importance, since when designing a compiler one frequently wishes to modify the grammar without modifying the language that the grammar generates. However, the general problem of deciding this for arbitrary context free grammars is undecidable. While this means that there cannot be any general algorithm that will answer this problem for arbitrary pairs of grammars, the determination whether two given grammars do generate the same language is done routinely, but may require a new method for different instances.

In particular, if the virus is known, it is not very difficult to design tests for software that will detect the presence or absence of that particular virus. This is one reason why it is important to obtain a copy of a virus as soon as possible after its detection. These tests will typically involve checking files for certain substrings that indicate the presence of a virus. Note that this is conceptually different from the process of purging a virus, as described in Section 10.2.

6.3 Bibliographical Note

The undecidability of detection is from [2].

Chapter Seven

Detection of Computer Viruses and Worms: Practical Aspects

This chapter is concerned with the question of how one can be warned that one's system is infected by a computer virus or worm. In view of the previous chapter, we concentrate mainly on observing symptoms. We will distinguish between observable symptoms of the spread of the attacker and the observable symptoms of any damage caused by the attacker. In both cases, there are symptoms that are more likely to be observed by an individual user of a system and those that are more likely to be detected by the system itself which has a global view of all users' domains.

7.1 Detection of Code

As we showed in the last chapter, it is not possible in general to determine whether a given program is, or contains, a virus. In practice however it is of course likely that careful inspection of the code will reveal whether a program appears suspicious. Typically one might look for unexpected or unexplained accesses to memory or to disk. Unfortunately, this type of inspection is bound to be *ad hoc* and cannot be completely formalized.

7.2 Symptoms of Spread

From our discussions, it should be clear that the major objective must always be to recognize any symptoms of the spread of an attacker, rather than symptoms of the damage that it has already caused. We distinguish between user observable symptoms and system observable symptoms of spread.

7.2.1 User Observable Symptoms of Spread

Many user observable symptoms have as a common characteristic the reduction of expected performance and consequences thereof. There are two groups, those relating to time and those relating to space.

In the time category, we have:

- *Changes in response time:* most users have a fairly good idea of the response time that they can expect, given a certain number of users on their system. This applies to shared systems with several users as well as to personal work stations where there is just one user who however may be executing several tasks at the same time. Any deviation (i.e., increase) in response time from the expected one should give cause for concern if no easy explanation is available. As indicated, viruses and worms will use the resources of a local computer to carry out self-replication (copying), auto-relocation (sending), and actions, including any tests to determine whether actions and/or self-replication should be delayed. Since this will reduce the computing resources available to the legitimate program, an observed sluggishness of the system could be due to an incipient infection.

- *Longer CPU times:* the increase in response time will be observable only in interactive sessions. For batch processing, the corresponding value is the CPU time. This is particularly useful in the case of programs that are repeatedly executed with similar data sets; therefore fairly reliable estimates of their execution times are available. Increases again should be viewed with suspicion as they could be symptoms of an infection. It should be noted however that batch processing systems tend to be more rigid (e.g., JCL must specify in considerable detail all files to be used, etc.) than interactive environments and are thus less prone to infection by viruses (and even less by worms).

As far as the space category of symptoms is concerned, we have:

- *Unexpected shortage of disk space:* (note that this applies only to virus attacks, as worms are not stored on disk.) It is useful to have a relatively precise idea of how much disk space a program occupies. This information could be kept in a separate file which is updated by the user whenever a file is changed. This information can then be used to provide an indication of an infection as follows. Before any use of a file, its actual size is determined and compared to the recorded size. If there is no discrepancy, the file should be the same as before (i.e., when the size was last determined and recorded), otherwise an infection should be suspected. This is based on the (very reasonable) assumption that the insertion of even the most simple virus will increase the size of the program. In extreme cases, e.g., if the virus is very large relative to the size of the infected programs or if the user's remaining free disk space was already precariously close to zero before the attempted infection by a virus, the attempted spread of the virus could very well result in exceeding the user's disk quota.

- *Unexpected shortage of memory:* this is the analogue of the previous scenario for main memory rather than for disk space; it now applies to worms as well as to viruses. A user may execute a program with known memory requirements. If the available memory is unexpectedly low, it could be an indication that the program has been infected.

- *Unexpectedly high number of page faults:* this is an obvious analogue of the previous scenario for a virtual memory environment. A virtual memory system gives the user the impression of providing a very large address space (main memory). It does this by keeping several smaller blocks of data (called pages) in physical main memory. When a memory reference is made by a statement in a program, the virtual memory system checks whether the referenced data element resides in one of the pages currently resident in main memory. If this is the case the reference is made; otherwise one of the memory resident pages is replaced by one that is retrieved from disk and does contain the requested data item. Retrieving a new page from disk is called a page fault. For a virtual memory organization to be efficient, locality of data references is desirable (i.e., if a page is retrieved, if possible all references to data in that page should occur at the same time in the program). A virus is likely to violate this requirement, and will thereby increase the number of page faults.

Another technique for detecting the spread of viruses is to record, possibly in a separate file to be updated by the user whenever a modification is made, the date of last change of a file. Since many virus programs are not sophisticated enough to prevent the system from updating the date of last change resulting from the insertion of the virus into the program, this can provide an indication of an infection. Even though this is an obvious variant of the technique of recording the size of a file, it should be noted that it is less reliable since virus programs are able, at least in principle, to prevent this system update.

Even the technique of recording the size is not completely fool-proof, since conceivably the virus could erase a portion of the program of the size of the virus; this however will most likely affect the overt behavior of the program, thereby indicating the presence of a major problem (although not necessarily of a virus). We note that strictly speaking the record of sizes or dates of last change should either be kept completely independent from the system or in a form that cannot be subverted. How this can be achieved will be discussed in a later chapter (Chapter 9).

7.2.2 System Observable Symptoms of Spread

System observable symptoms (observed either automatically or manually, by systems personnel) clearly contain all those that can be observed by the individual users:

- Unexpected shortage of disk space.
- Unexpected shortage of memory.
- Unexpectedly high number of page faults.

However, there are other symptoms that ordinarily would not be accessible to users. Among them are:

- *Unexplainably high bus traffic:* if the internal bus traffic is higher than that which would be expected given the currently executing tasks, the spread of a virus or worm might be the cause.

- *Unexpectedly high incoming/outgoing mail traffic:* since the mail system is the usual avenue for sending attackers over networks, this can provide an early indication of a worm or virus spread.

- *Unusually high numbers of unsuccessful or incomplete log-ins:* this is usually an indication of an attempted break-in. Possible reactions might be trace backs (to find out where the attempts originated) and disabling the link or network connection.

- *Deviation of user behavior from user profiles:* for this method it is assumed that the systems have available a profile of each user; this can be either manually input or compiled from past behavior. Any substantial deviation of the actually observed behavior from the behavior expected according to the user profile could be considered suspicious. For example, a very unsophisticated user might suddenly use systems services; a user who has never sent any mail anywhere suddenly decides to swamp the user community with his messages. These are clear warning signals to a system that suspicious activities are performed and should result in notification of the systems manager and subsequent follow-up.

Attempted illegal operations: while this is self-evident, it is not likely to occur with a correct virus or worm. This is because a worm or virus usually does not violate access privileges in an overt way. Rather it subverts a program and then (ab)uses this host to carry out accesses that are perfectly legal for the host. However, if the attacker uses a flaw that had previously been fixed at the installation, it is not difficult to arm this now proscribed access path with an alarm that then indicates an attempted attack. For example, if the Gnu-Emacs editor in a particular system had been modified to not permit files to be moved into the system area (see Chapter 5), a simple extension of this modification could be to trap any attempts to perform such operations and then disable the account from which the attempt was made.

Other techniques are possible, depending on the particular system and the use made of it. One might be to prevent any changes of files containing executable or object code; the only way in which such a file could legally be created according to this scheme is by a compiler or linker. This is of course based on the assumption that compiler and linker are not subverted; if they are this approach is of no use.

The most likely symptom for the system is however provided by:

- *Extensive, and usually rather abruptly starting, complaints by users about perceived symptoms of spread.* These must be treated carefully, as (initially at least) the complaints are likely to be rather nonspecific and will appear unrelated to any infection. Clearly, it will be counterproductive to suspect a virus everytime one user reports some type of problem. However, on the other hand, the earlier an actual virus infection is detected, the less damage will occur.

7.3 Symptoms of Damage

The obvious problem here is how to distinguish between the damage done by a virus or worm program and the result of a programming error or operating system or compiler bug. In most cases, there will be no easy answer. Until very recently, a significant reluctance can be observed to accept the existence of a virus or worm when unexplained disappearances of files occur. This is because the power of these attackers has not been adequately assessed or accepted. Undoubtedly, this will change sooner or later and will then be replaced by a tendency to 'blame it on a virus'. Generally, it is likely that the determination of the existence of an infection must be done by the system rather than an individual user; by the very nature of viruses and worms, entire communities are infected rather than single user domains, and therefore the problem of detecting and combatting by necessity is one of the system.

Clearly, from a user point of view, the obvious symptoms are:

- Unexplained aborts of program executions.
- Hung systems, requiring rebooting of the system.

Other symptoms are changes in files, without destroying the entire file. This can be detected by comparing the recorded date of last change as described in Section 7.2.1.

From the system point of view, the obvious symptoms are:

- Wide-spread user consternation (at the very least) about their problems (see above).
- Attempted illegal operations, as outlined in Section 7.2.2.

7.4 Detection Products

There are several products available, both commercially and from bulletin boards, which were written to protect users who are concerned about the threat from viruses. Since it cannot be the intent of this book to endorse any product or determine whether a product works, we merely give brief descriptions of the methods that are used in some of these products.

- Interception of all calls to the BIOS code in read-only memory (ROM) as a program is run (see Section 4.3). The program's execution is halted before any such call is executed and the anticipated consequences of its execution are displayed. The user can then decide whether to execute the call or to abort it.
- Interception of certain interrupt calls (13H and 26H) which are frequently used by virus programs.
- Reporting possibly dangerous disk activities such as formatting a disk. This information is communicated to the user in ways that reduce the likelihood of being intercepted by any attacker.

- Computing a cryptographic checksum of files which can be used to verify the integrity of a program before execution.

- Computing a program authentication code (PAC) also using an encryption scheme. At regular intervals, this detection program reprocesses the executable program and determines another PAC. If this PAC and the previously determined PAC match, it is assumed that no virus infection has occurred up to this point. (This approach assumes that the original program was not infected.)

- Adding hardware protection to intercept unwanted write commands.

Some approaches will be covered in more detail in Chapter 9.

7.5 Bibliographical Notes

[47] contains a survey of several virus protection products, including addresses of vendors. [48] is a preliminary technical evaluation and assessment of a virus protection program for the IBM PC, XT or AT, or compatible system.

PART IV

PREVENTION AND CURES

In the last part (III), *a-priori* detection of viruses and their actions was discussed. This part (IV) deals with a related but different scenario: assuming that viruses exist in a system, what can be done to limit their spread and eliminate them from the system.

Chapter Eight

Prevention: Theoretical Aspects

In this chapter, we discuss the theoretical limits of prevention. In particular, we show that it is very difficult to prevent viruses. We discuss the implications of these results and look at schemes for classifying information. We postpone the discussion of practical considerations until the next chapter.

8.1 Prevention of Viruses

Prevention refers to the ability to ensure that an uninfected system remains uninfected. While this is a very desirable property, it turns out to be rather difficult, if not impossible, to achieve it.

We note that the ability to keep a system uninfected is a necessary but not a sufficient requirement for data integrity. The problem lies in the difficulty of determining at what point in time the system was uninfected. Because viruses can lie dormant arbitrarily long, it is practically impossible to ascertain whether a system is uninfected. It is also theoretically impossible, since this ability would be equivalent to detection which we already know to be undecidable. Thus, one assumes that a system was uninfected at a certain point and attempts to prevent any subsequent infections.

There is one certain method that guarantees prevention, and that is isolation. In other words, if no new programs are ever introduced into a system, then no virus can be introduced either. We use the term program here in the sense of anything that can eventually be executed. However, this is practically infeasible, since it assumes that no software can be maintained (since this would entail modifying existing, and thereby creating new, software) and no new software can be developed.

A relaxation of this very extreme approach is to assume that one can trust one's own staff, but others can not be trusted. This implies that no programs can be shared with outsiders, since viruses can be propagated through sharing.

A further relaxation of these ideas then leads to flow controls. Here limits are imposed on the paths that information can take. Obviously, the last two methods can be formulated in terms of flow restrictions. There are two models that are of relevance here, the Biba model and the Bell-LaPadula model. In the Biba model every piece of information has an associated integrity level, in the Bell-LaPadula model every piece of information has a security level. The two are duals to each other. In the Biba model, no user at a given integrity level can read an object of a lower integrity level nor write an object at a higher integrity level; in the Bell-LaPadula model, no user at a given security level can read an object at a higher security level nor read an object at a lower security level. The two models can be combined, giving rise to a variety of combinations. The Bell-LaPadula model causes all information to move up in the security hierarchy, while the Biba model causes all information to move down in the integrity hierarchy. The objective of these models is to create restricted classes of information which can be accessed only by members of a certain level.

While some of these considerations may be applicable in very special, usually very static, situations, it is safe to say that most computing installations could not operate under the restrictions imposed by either one of the two models, and even less under their combination.

8.2 Hardware Modifications

A fundamental problem in guarding against viruses and worms is the question how to prevent a piece of code from writing information on a file. It is easy to see that most approaches that rely on software can be subverted.

This explains the attraction of hardware schemes; where software is logical and flexible by definition and can therefore be manipulated relatively easily and moreover remotely, hardware is inflexible and impossible to change if one is not physically present. There are several proposals that are ultimately based on the premise that hardware cannot be manipulated remotely. While they are quite effective in guarding against viruses, it is not very likely that they will be implemented in the near future. These will be sketched in the next chapter.

8.3 Bibliographical Notes

The discussion of flow controls as a means of guarding against viruses is taken from [2]. Data flow techniques are discussed in [2]; the notion of limiting spread, defined in [3], had been introduced earlier in [49], [50] and [51]. Some approaches based on the imperviousness of hardware to remote manipulation are given in [52] and [53].

Chapter Nine

Prevention of Virus Attacks: Practical Aspects

In this chapter we move on to the practical aspects of attempting to guard against attacks by viruses. We sketch several methods, along with a critical assessment of their practicality and difficulty of implementation. Our starting point is that we believe our system has been invaded and we wish to prevent the spread of the virus in order to minimize possible damage to our system's files.

9.1 Software - Based Protection Schemes

The schemes listed below are implemented using software; as pointed out in Section 8.2, any type of software is subject to subversion. Therefore, special attention must be paid to the integrity of software that is designed to protect the integrity of other software and data. In fact, the integrity of the most sensitive file in the entire system is no greater than the integrity of the protection software.

A major complication in detecting and preventing viruses is their tendency to infect primarily executable code. Modifications of executable code are far less noticeable than modification of other data or program files; therefore executable code is a primary target for viruses. In extreme cases, this can be exploited by not permitting any executable code in media that can be easily written. While this may be a very drastic approach, it is possible that it can be combined with some of the other approaches described below to make infection very difficult.

- *Restrictive system defaults.* A very simple way of increasing the immunity of any system is to have the

81

system administrator set appropriate default protection codes for files. If these are set so that by default no files can be executed unless specifically requested, the spread of viruses may be greatly impeded. While it will not provide a fool-proof protection mechanism, it limits the ways in which viruses can spread and helps in tracking their progress, with the ultimate objective of determining their source.

- *Requiring separate and explicit approval (from the user) for certain operations, usually write operations of some form, including formatting disks.* This assumes an interactive environment and may be too cumbersome for many applications. Technically, this can be implemented either as software that requires the user to enter an approval code or as a hardware device attached to a disk drive that prevents unapproved writes to that disk. The approval for the hardware device can be via a simple push button physically located on the device. For the software protection mechanism, the approval procedure is more difficult to protect, since in contrast to the hardware device which is not under the control of the operating system of the computer, the software implementing this approach may itself be already subverted or else the approval code might be intercepted and copied if it is relatively unsophisticated. It may be necessary to use here a general authentication scheme (see Appendix) which makes this approach even more laborious. Another problem is that even if the user can control every write to disk, the user is probably not in a position to make a correct assessment whether the writes are in fact only the legitimate writes or whether there are other, subversive writes hidden among the legitimate ones.

- *Comparison with a protected copy.* Here the assumption is that there exists a permanent, up-to-date, trusted copy of the file which is stored either in encrypted form or in write-once memory. The method of guarding against infiltration consists of a comparison of that file with the conventionally stored copy whenever there are doubts about the integrity of the latter. This is relatively easy to implement. However, there is some question whether a permanent, up-to-date, trusted copy exists. If it were so easy to satisfy this requirement it might be preferable to execute this program in the first place, instead of the possibly infected copy.

- *Control key.* A control key can be computed for each file. This may be some type of check sum, the length of the file, or some other function of the file. Again, it is imperative that this control key be stored incorruptibly. This can be done in a variety of ways, for example by using encryption in conjunction with some redundancy or by using write-once memory. Also of importance might be that the computation of the control key should be relatively fast, since otherwise users will sacrifice security to convenience. This is very easy to implement.

- *Time stamping.* Many operating systems store a date of last modification for each file together with other information. If a user stores separately and either incorruptibly in the system or altogether outside of the system the date of the last modification that was done by the user, discrepancies can indicate possible infiltrations. As indicated, viruses have in principle the ability of preventing a change in the date of last modification caused by the insertion of the virus code into a program, but those viruses that have been seen have not done this. This method requires a certain amount of discipline on the part of the users, which may well doom it.

- *Encryption.* Files can be stored in encrypted form. Before any usage, a file must be decrypted. Any insertion of unencrypted code (as it would be done by a virus trying to infiltrate a binary) will give garbage when the resulting file is decrypted. Again, it is important to ensure that the decryption program cannot be subverted. For if it were subverted, it could simply ignore the portion that corresponds to the virus and decrypt only the rest of the (now successfully subverted) binary. The method itself is easy to implement; the protection of the decryption software is somewhat more difficult.

- *Write-once disks.* This is an application of a hardware feature that guarantees data integrity. While in principle, commonly used codes such as ASCII can be changed when used on write-once (or laser or digital optical) disks, it is unlikely that such an attempt will be successful for

83

the purpose of creating a virus (the changes one can obtain from ASCII are very limited); furthermore, there exist so-called immutable codes for which it can be guaranteed that changes are impossible. This is probably an approach that is preferable to having an encrypted copy, since here much less work is to be done in comparing copies. Write-once disks are also attractive for storing control keys incorruptibly. For a discussion of write-once disks and of immutable codes, see the Appendix.

All these methods attempt to prevent unauthorized changes in programs or data. The protected copy, control key, and write-once memory schemes work primarily in a very static environment where little or no changes occur (most production environments). The time-stamping and encryption methods can also be applied if changes are to be possible.

It should be noted that schemes that require explicit user approval for certain write or update operations operate outside of ordinary access controls. It should be quite clear that even the most sophisticated discretionary access controls (DACs) are powerless when it comes to dealing with viruses: DACs are designed to prevent outsiders from accessing privileged data; the problem is that a virus, once it has infected a user's software, is no longer an outsider, but rather an insider. DACs have no way to prevent access by insiders. While some have criticized this as a flaw of DACs, this criticism is invalid; DACs were never designed to deal with strictly internal threats and should not be faulted for that. It is however conceivable to modify DACs so that even internally admissible accesses require explicit approval in certain cases; this would have to be done along the lines sketched above.

Encryption methods have one additional advantage, namely that illicit modifications of programs can even be detected outside the realm of a particular security/integrity environment. This is of particular interest for software distribution. While it is true that software could be mailed to clients on write-once media (WORM disks), this is a rather cumbersome method;

furthermore, recipients would have to have hardware available that permits them to read these disks. It is much more convenient to send software by electronic mail or similar data links. However, here the danger of subversion looms. Using encryption, this can be effectively avoided since the key is usually small enough that it can be transmitted in alternative ways. Thus, even if an executable program is modified "in transit", this modification can be detected by the recipient before the subverted code is ever executed.

None of the outlined methods will guarantee that every attempted infiltration will be foiled. However, they may make it very difficult for a virus to defeat the security defenses of a computer installation. One side effect of complicated defenses is that the methods for evading the defense mechanisms tend to be complicated as well. This implies that the virus will become larger, thereby increasing the likelihood that it will be spotted.

Note, however, that all these defense mechanisms are geared toward permanently stored files. Thus, they will be ineffective in guarding against worms. As we saw in our discussion of the Internet Worm, it employed techniques that were somewhat different from those of the viruses we discussed.

9.2 Hardware - Based Protection Schemes

There are several schemes that utilize hardware with the objective of preventing the spread of a virus infection. These are of varying complexity, from rather simple to enormously complex; their effect on system usability and efficiency of execution vary drastically, as well.

We have already mentioned (in Section 9.1) the hardware implementation of separate and explicit approval for certain write operations. As a very low-tech variation on this scheme, it is trivial to write-protect ordinary floppy disks simply by removing the tab that allows writes. For very disciplined users it may be possible to use this device to create a class of programs that are trusted which can be used to compare exposed copies.

Alternatively, if writes occur very infrequently this copy can be used for reads and executes. However, this requires that every file, before it is written to such a disk, be carefully inspected for the presence of viruses.

Several comprehensive hardware schemes have been proposed with the purpose of preventing viruses. One of them in particular would require a complete change in hardware, both architectually and in implementation. The system is in essence a hardware implementation of capability systems; note that the problems with DACs that we mentioned above (Section 9.1) are no longer present since the hardware rigidly governs access and even insiders are only permitted to modify programs but not the capabilities associated with them. (The capabilities are assigned by the hardware).

This proposal solves, according to its author, all known software-based internal computer security problems including those caused by Trojan horse and virus programs. This comes at a price. The hardware modifications are enormous; in particular there is a large internal memory accessible only to the hardware to enable it to administer the capabilities associated with instructions. Each instruction is greatly enlarged in order to transport and assist in managing the capabilities associated with it. Each instruction is prefixed with a protection domain identifier created by the hardware. The program domain is viewed in the proposal as composed of many small protection domains, each with its own unique protection domain identifier, proposed to be 16 bits long. Since domains can be nested, the hardware maintains a table in its own private memory of active and inactive protection domain identifiers. Four bits are added to the instruction to represent its type; in particular, executable operation, port, and capability are distinguished here. Then comes the original instruction. Finally, four additonal bits are appended, representing the access rights involved, one for each of read, write, destroy, and copy-self accesses. Since all additional fields in this greatly expanded instruction can only be modified by the hardware, which is assumed unsubvertable, it can now be shown that this results in a computer architecture in which security and integrity risks are greatly reduced, if not completely eliminated.

To verify this claim for a virus one can see that although it may still be possible to design a virus, this virus would probably not function, since during compiling and loading the architecture will create a protection domain identifier table for it, using its own private memory. This table is based on the information contained in the added fields of each instruction, which are neither visible nor otherwise accessible outside of the custom hardware. In the virus's attempt to spread itself to another program, the hardware would detect the attempt to go outside of the allocated protection domain, thus foiling the virus.

It is clear, just from our short sketch, that substantial overhead is entailed; a 24-bit instruction has doubled in length, a major capability system must be implemented in hardware, and nested protection domains must be administered. However, the author claims it is all worth it because hardware is becoming less expensive, and therefore the price of eliminating "all known software-based internal computer security problems" "is approaching some 'affordable' figure".

While such a scheme may be acceptable to the military (the employer of the proposal's author), it is hoped that civilians will never have to resort to such drastic approaches in order to be able to "compute in peace".

9.3 Bibliographical Notes

The paper [54] gives a survey of virus defense mechanisms. Also of interest are [55], [56] and [57], as well as [42], [47], [53], [36] and [3]. In particular, [57] defines an interesting notion of risk levels; unfortunately it appears that in order to make this system practical, certain ways of circumventing this scheme must be provided (the "RUN-UNTRUSTED" feature) which make the scheme less attractive. The major architectural modification is proposed in [52]. A significantly reduced variant of this proposal, reduced both in complexity and overhead and also in resulting security and integrity, is contained in [53]. Both proposals are somewhat related to a proposal contained in [58], where a cryptoregister, designed for software protection, had similar functions and requirements as the private hardware of [52] and the hard-code kernel and security specialist of [53]. General authentication schemes are discussed in [58]; digital optical disks, immutable codes, and their applications to data integrity are studied in [59].

Chapter Ten

Cures

In Chapter 6 we showed that it is not possible to determine in general whether a given program contains a virus. This is clearly a disappointing and troubling result. Mainly, it stems from the generality of the problem that we posed, namely determining whether any virus is present. Since detection in general is not possible, we may want to determine how to purge a virus once a system is infected. Also of interest are schemes to undo any damages caused by the attacker.

10.1 Undoing Damages

Undoing primary damages is difficult. If files have been erased, the only way to recover from this loss is if there are up-to-date back-up copies available. It is crucial to be certain that these back-up copies are clean, i.e., uninfected, as otherwise the attacker may strike again later. It should also be kept in mind that most attackers have built-in delays; so even if no primary action can be observed now, this does not guarantee that no damage will occur later.

Secondary damages are mainly due to unchecked replication; here the scheme outlined below (Section 10.2) may provide some help if the attacker is known. If sensitive data have been divulged (the scenario where the attacker infiltrates a file in order to transmit data or programs for purposes of espionage; see Section 3.6.2), it is impossible to get the information back.

10.2 Purging an Attacker

Assuming an attacker is known in detail (see Section 4.4.5 for example), it may be possible to purge it from a system by using the following scheme. Note that this will be particularly useful if, because of time delays, little or no primary damage has been caused, but there is reason to believe that major damage will eventually ensue.

The approach consists of releasing a modification of the virus or worm in the system, which is designed to combat actively the existing attacker. It must have the following properties:

(a) It searches for copies of the original attacker; this can be done using an inversion of the method for preventing reinfection. Typically, to guard against reinfection, the attacker tests whether a certain value resides in a certain position. If this is the case, no further infection is carried out; otherwise the system is infected and the position is set to the specified value. This can of course be turned around to permit the modified attacker (counter-attacker) to detect the original attacker.

(b) The counter-attacker's only primary action is to erase all of the original attacker, except for the values that guard against reinfection. This prevents the attacker from reinfecting the code again.

(c) The counter-attacker erases itself from the system after a certain date. This approach should be used primarily if it is too cumbersome to use any other and if the attacker is clearly malicious.

Extreme care must be taken in letting the counter-attacker loose; it is strongly recommended to test this procedure first on an isolated portion of the computer network, containing files that can easily be recovered. This approach is similar to that employed in searching for and destroying worm programs (see Section 2.1).

We remark that some attackers (typically all worms) reside only in memory and are never permanently stored. In these cases it is of course sufficient to turn the system off (power the system down) to erase the attacker. This may not be very easy in the case where the system is a large network. For example, the Internet Worm would have been permanently erased if all (approximately 60,000) nodes had been turned off for a few minutes at the same time. Clearly a single node that does not participate can defeat this approach.

Chapter Eleven

Precautionary Rules of Thumb

In this last chapter we list several rules which point out more or less obvious precautions that one should take. These are primarily geared towards a business environment. In all cases, it is important that the situation is explained and that reasons are given why certain measures are taken. This is all the more necessary as it is impossible to supervise employees at all times in order to ensure that rules are followed. It is therefore imperative that employees understand rules and in consequence accept them. While the threat posed by viruses should not be overdramatized, employees must understand that it is a serious threat.

(1) Employees must understand the potential danger viruses and worms present. They must be aware that they may lose their jobs if an attack occurs because of their negligence.

(2) No outside programs must be installed on any company system (including PCs and personal work stations) without going first through a formal (and preferably central) review and testing procedure. Only those programs formally authorized in the review and testing procedure should be used on the system. The only exception could be programs that were written internally and from scratch. In particular, programs downloaded from electronic bulletin boards or received via electronic mail must not be used under any circumstances, unless they have been formally reviewed and tested. This rule applies also to

(3) University disks for doing homework and assignments on company equipment. If the company does want to allow its employees to use its equipment, it is safer to provide off-line systems for this use which then

must not be used for business purposes or only after cold-boots with different diskettes and reformatted hard disks, if any exist.

(4) The company systems must not be interfaced directly with any electronic bulletin boards. Stand-alone systems with very limited and carefully controlled connections to the other systems should be used for this purpose. The same applies also to receiving electronic mail.

(5) If at all possible, software should be accepted only as source code. Furthermore, if the source code appears suspicious (e.g., accesses ports for no apparent reason), extra care should be taken. In other words, just because a program is in source code this does not guarantee it to be free of viruses.

(6) All files, including system software, must be periodically and reliably backed up. Back up copies may have to be kept much longer than one would retain them ordinarily, depending on the value of the files that could be destroyed by an attacker and the perceived vulnerability of the system. As indicated, there is no guarantee that back up files are uninfected, but in the worst case an infected copy is still better than an erased one.

(7) Protection should be set on all files. In particular, if legitimate use of some file implies read-only access this should be enforced.

(8) System default values should be set restrictively.

(9) Some of the more complicated techniques outlined in Chapter 9 should be considered, even if the ultimate decision is against their implementation.

(10) All security policies should be reviewed periodically with an eye towards improving constraints and adding controls. Particular attention must be paid to the enforcement of existing regulations; it is more important to enforce existing rules that are enforceable than to create new ones that again may not be enforced.

Chapter Twelve
Conclusions

There is no question that computer viruses and similar attackers of the integrity of software and data present the most serious threat to computer security that exists today. This is on the one hand because so many different systems are at risk and on the other hand because a truly vicious virus could cause very substantial damage.

However, the response to this threat should not be blind panic.

In this book we have reviewed a large number of different attackers, with the aim of providing some insight into how these attacks are carried out. We have then drawn conclusions how one can impede, if not prevent, these attacks. These techniques range from very simple to very complicated and affect customary data processing operations in various ways.

We believe that the first step in countering the threat posed by computer viruses consists of educating all computer users, including system personnel, of the threat, emphasizing how infiltrations occur and establishing rapid notification procedures as well as responsibilities in case of a presumed attack. It has been repeatedly demonstrated that rapid response is crucial to a successful recovery. It was also found to be very beneficial to have formally established a fall-back plan that must be activated as soon as things get out of hand. This planning process combined with heightened awareness of the threat should be sufficient to deal with most threats, especially if many or all users are involved in it.

It must be kept in mind that the more onerous a method, the more likely it will be circumvented. In fact, the truly rigid and crippling rules will tempt some of the more creative employees to devise virus techniques that prove that even these rules do not protect against viruses. This would then result in precisely the opposite of what was intended with them. Thus we recommend common sense and the golden rule **'do unto others as you want them to do unto you'** - in other words, people who formulate protection policies should ask themselves how they felt about them if they had to work with the resulting system.

Basic Hygiene

- Viruses and worms are serious threats. Negligence in dealing with this threat may endanger jobs.

- Be aware of this threat. Notify designated personnel if you suspect a virus or a worm affecting the system.

- Do not use or install outside programs of any kind that have not been formally reviewed. This includes programs on disks for homework for university or training courses.

- Except for designated stand-alone systems, never interface any company systems directly with any electronic bulletin boards.

- Except for designated stand-alone systems, never receive outside electronic mail on any company systems.

- Always attempt to install software in source code only.

- Always set protection on all files in the safest (i.e., most restrictive) way. In particular, all object files must be read-only.

- Always keep adequate back-up copies.

- Make sure you know and understand the established procedure to be carried out in case of an emergency. This includes names and telephone numbers of designated personnel to call (office and home), both during regular business hours as well as at night and during weekends. Be aware that electronic mail may not work during an emergency.

Appendix

In this appendix we will briefly summarize three different topics that were referred to in various places in the main body of this book. They are relatively disjointed and no attempt is made to connect them logically. They are:

- Authorization systems
- Cryptography
- Write-once disks

A1. Authorization Systems

A1.A. Introduction

The concept of authorization is central to any manipulation of data where privacy or secrecy of information is of relevance. The basic question is, "Who may do what with which data object?" In this section we will assume the following situation. Any user of a data object has certain rights to it. We will discuss how such rights or privileges may be acquired, how they may be passed on to other users, how such grants may be revoked, and how a user may determine whether there is a possibility that another user in a given situation can exercise a certain right to this object. Therefore we are concerned with the granting, the revoking, and the administration of privileges.

In order to simplify the presentation we make several assumptions:

1. *Users are what they appear to be.* Thus we assume that we have a correctly working user identification procedure and that each user can be unmistakeably identified. This implies that the software performing the identification process works correctly and cannot be subverted. It also implies that only the real user A can

identify himself as user A. Thus we assume that any attempt by any user other than A at pretending to be A can be detected. (In the section on applications of cryptography of this appendix, A2.C.2, we discuss ways to implement such a mechanism.)

2. *The software system is correct and secure.* Correctness means that the system performs exactly as stated in its formal specification. However, this does not mean that the system is secure, since there is no guarantee that the formal specification reflects precisely the intentions of the designer. Clearly these difficulties increase with the size and complexity of the software system. Hence it is interesting that there exist provably secure operating systems. Although they are relatively primitive and highly inefficient, the fact that it is possible to write such systems justifies our assumption.

3. The hardware, software, and data are adequately physically protected. This can be achieved by traditional means and is of no interest here.

Our main objective then is to determine within a given framework whether a user is authorized to access a data object and, if not, how to prevent this unauthorized access. A user for our purposes is any entity which acts on data objects, and a data object may be anything stored in some computer-accessible medium. Since both user and data object may be programs, the names "user" and "data object" imply only the direction of an action. In this approach to data security, the passing, or flow, of control becomes more important than the mere access to data. A security analysis of an authorization system is then an analysis of its flow of control. That such an analysis can be quite nontrivial can be seen from the following trivial program fragment

```
        if x ≠ 0 then goto L;
        print(0);
    L:  print(1)
```

While it is obvious that this program will indicate whether $x = 0$, it is by no means easy to formulate general and sufficiently precise rules according to which this program is detected as a potential security risk if the value of x is to be kept secret. One (partial) approach to this problem is the usual military policy for classifying information. Underlying it is a two-dimensional hierarchy of security classes (i,a), with the component i being the authority level and the component a the category. Typical authority levels are confidential $(i = 1)$, secret $(i = 2)$, and top secret $(i = 3)$. A category consists of one or more compartments, typically unrestricted $(a = u)$, restricted $(a = r)$, sensitive $(a = s)$, and crypto $(a = c)$. Information can be passed from user A with security class (i, a) to user B with security class (j, b) if and only if B's authority level is no lower than A's $(i \leq j)$ and every compartment associated with A is also associated with B $(a \subseteq b)$. Several computer systems are based on this scheme. The Bell-LaPadula *-property is an interesting variant; if a user has the read privilege to an object A and the write privilege to another object B, it postulates that the security class of A be dominated by that of B (cf. Section 8.1).

There are serious problems with these approaches:

1. Overclassification of information. Information will always move upward in the hierarchy and never downward. Thus, after some time much information will be overclassified.

2. Lack of generality. For example, it can easily be seen that for every possible security class there must be a separate sorting procedure.

A1.B. The Safety Problem

The safety problem is contained in the question of whether a user A can ever get access to a data object X. Clearly this question is of interest in the presence of several users, i.e., if resources are shared. In particular, this applies to networks. It turns out that the operations of a realistic access control system are sufficiently powerful to render the safety problem undecidable. For more details, we refer to the literature.

A1.C. An Implementation

It is instructive to give a brief overview of a commercially available database, System R. Objects in this database system are of three kinds, namely data objects, communication objects, and transaction objects. Data objects are physical files and views. A physical file may be a program or a database. A view is a dynamic window based on one or more physical files and defines a certain way of looking at these files. A view can be used to let a user see only certain fields or combinations of fields but not the complete file. For instance, a user of census files may get access to a view which shows the combined family income divided by the size of the household (per capita income for each household) without having access to either of the two fields of the physical file. Since a view must reflect changes in a file instantaneously, it is necessary to recompute the view every time it is used. Consequently, views are distinguished from files in the way they are authorized: the creator of a physical file always has all rights to this file as a matter of policy. The definer of a view does not, as the rights to the view depend on the rights which the user has to the underlying file(s).

Communication objects are logical ports and message queues. Transaction objects are parametrized programs performing operations on data objects and communication objects. They are of no concern in our considerations as long as they exist and function properly.

Usage of the objects is governed by the following rules. Each user can use only those objects for which that user has proper authorization. A user who creates a new object holds all rights to it (except for views, as noted above). Objects can be shared only if the owner grants explicit permission. Every right can be granted in one of two versions in System R, with grant-option and without grant-option. In the first case (with grant-option) the user to whom the privilege was granted is free to grant the right to other users (even with grant-option again) while retaining the right himself. In the second case (without grant-option), the recipient cannot grant the privilege in turn to another user.

The following are the major privileges which can be granted:

READ: the recipient can use the object in a query; this privilege permits reading items from the file and defining views.

INSERT: the recipient can insert new items into the file.

DELETE: the recipient can delete items in the file.

UPDATE: the recipient can modify existing items in the file; this privilege may be restricted to certain items or to certain fields in the file.

DROP: the recipient can delete the entire file from the system.

EXECUTE: the recipient can execute a file (program).

As an example, let us assume that user A is the creator of the file EMPLOYEE and suppose that the following commands are issued:

```
A:  GRANT READ, INSERT
    ON EMPLOYEE TO B
    WITH GRANT-OPTION
A:  GRANT READ
    ON EMPLOYEE TO X
    WITH GRANT-OPTION
B:  GRANT READ, INSERT
    ON EMPLOYEE TO X
```

Note that all grants are supported by the requisite authorization. If this is not the case, a grant is ignored. After the three commands are executed, user X has the right READ with grant-option from A and the right INSERT without grant-option from B.

Every time a grant is issued, the authorization module verifies whether the grant is authorized. If it is, the successful grant is recorded for testing whether a user may exercise or grant a certain privilege.

Authorization on views is not as simple as that on files. As pointed out, the creator of a physical file is fully and solely authorized to perform actions on it. The creator of a view, on the other hand is solely but not fully authorized, for views are defined on the basis of files and thus the authorization on a user's view depends on that user's authorization on the underlying files.

Any user who has granted a privilege may subsequently revoke it. Furthermore, if a grantor revokes a privilege from some recipient, the authorization mechanism must then also revoke all those privileges which originated in the now revoked right. Thus, in the example above, if the command

A: REVOKE INSERT
    ON EMPLOYEE FROM B

is issued by A, not only will B lose the INSERT right but X will lose it as well, since its INSERT privilege originated in the now revoked grant from A to B. On the other hand, if the READ privilege instead of the INSERT privilege had been revoked in that command, X would not have lost its READ right, since it still holds the grant from A.

Formally, the meaning of the REVOKE command is defined as follows. Suppose

$$\sigma = G_1 \ G_2 \ \cdots \ G_{i\text{-}1} \ G_i \ G_{i+1} \ \cdots \ G_n$$

in a sequence of grants, where each G_j is a grant of a single privilege, written down in the temporal order in which the grants were issued (i.e., if G_x occurred before G_y, then $x < y$). Now suppose G_i is revoked by a command R_i. Then the meaning of the sequence

$$\sigma \ R_i$$

is identical to that of the following sequence:

$$G_1 \ G_2 \ \cdots \ G_{i\text{-}1} \ G_i \ G_{i+1} \ \cdots \ G_n$$

Note that a grant which is not supported by the required authorization is simply ignored. This implies that any (in fact, all) of the grants G_{i+1} through G_n may now not be properly authorized and may thus be ignored.

Figures A1 and A2 illustrate that it may not be obvious to determine which grants must be revoked. If A revokes the grant to B in Figure A1, X and C retain the right, but B, D and E lose it.

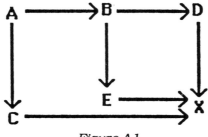

Figure A1.

In Figure A2, if A revokes the grant to B, all of B, C, D, E, and X lose it.

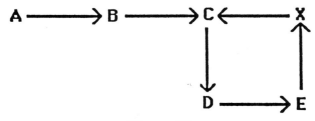

Figure A2.

Figure A3 shows that in the presence of revocation it is not sufficient to record only who got what privilege from whom; it is also necessary to record at what time t the grant was made:

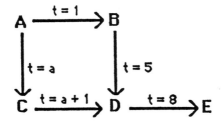

Figure A3.

where a is an integer variable. Assume that A revokes the grant to B. Thus B's grant to D is also revoked. Whether the grant from D to E must be revoked depends on the time $t = a$ of A's grant to C: if a ≤ 6, D will have received the grant from C in time to support its grant to E, namely before time $t = 8$, even though B's grant to D is revoked. On the other hand, if $a > 7$, the grant from C is received by D at a time at least 9, or too late to be able to support D's grant to E; thus this grant must be revoked.

It is clear that authorization checking must be done at run time. Revocation can become quite expensive since one grant (the one to be revoked) may provide the support for many other grants (which then must also be revoked).

A1.D. Bounded Propagation of Privileges

Users may be interested in the question of how far privileges can propagate. More specifically, if A is the creator of a file F, A will have a legitimate interest in knowing how many other users hold privileges to F at some point in time - legitimate since all these privileges directly or indirectly originated from grants by A. A related question is through how many "hands" the privilege passed before it ended up at some user B. Both questions are natural and of practical interest. The first question is concerned with the total number of users holding a right to an object. The second question deals with the length of the chain of grants which enables B to exercise a privilege; to see its practical importance, bear in mind that most people are quite willing to trust a friend, they are less confident in trusting a friend's friend, and very few would be willing to extend the same trust to a friend's friend of a friend's friend! Note that this last situation corresponds precisely to a length of 4 in the chain of "trusting someone".

It is not difficult to answer both questions in the given authorization system. However, because of our original motivation, the user may be interested not only in getting answers to these questions, but also in imposing limits which are then automatically enforced by the system, something the authorization mechanism of System R does not support. More specifically, suppose A creates F and passes some right r on F to B. When passing r to B, A also sends a nonnegative integer q, called the propagation number, which has the following significance: B can pass r on to other users only if the propagation number q is not 0 ($q > 0$); if q is 0, B may exercise r but cannot pass it on to others. Furthermore, the propagation number of a recipient is always at least 1 less than that of the grantor. This guarantees that the creator of an object can bound the length of the longest chain or privileges simply by granting the rights with a propagation number no greater than the desired maximal length. This mechanism can be implemented very easily.

Imposing a limit on the total number of users who may hold a privilege to an object can be done analogously; in this case the propagation number would reflect the remaining number of recipients who can still be given the right. There is, however, a difference; that is, at some point a user may have exhausted his propagation number and is unable to make further grants. For example, if B received the right r with $q = 6$ and B granted r to C with $q = 4$ and to D with $q = 1$, then B will not be able to make any further grants, as $6 = 4 + 1 + 1$ (where the last 1 comes from the fact that B is a recipient too). Thus B could continue granting only if B received an additional grant or recovered some grants by revoking them.

A2. Cryptosystems

Suppose we want to prevent unauthorized users from attaining access to our data. Operating systems are notoriously unsafe, and systems programmers typically have fairly unrestricted access anyway. Therefore the assumption made in authorization systems that users without explicit authorization do not gain access may be untenable in certain cases. Consequently, it is usually not possible to guarantee that access is prevented. What we can do, however, is make certain that nobody without proper authorization can "understand" our data. This can be achieved by encrypting the data in such a way that only users who know how to decrypt can get access to the meaning of the data; all others, even though they may get access, will not be in a positon to extract the information hidden in the encrypted data. Since encryption is a very important approach for achieving data protection, we will discuss several different methods.

Virtually all encryption schemes are based on keys. While it is conceivable that the general encryption method itself is secret, this is usually an assumption which will hold only for a relatively short time and even then only if the group of participants in the exchange of secret information is small. This is certainly not an assumption one should make in connection with data security; hence we will assume that the general methods for encryption and decryption are known and that the keys are the input which is variable and secret. As a consequence, one method may have a large number of implementations, each of which corresponds to a different key.

One distinguishes two fundamentally different schemes, namely symmetric encryption and asymmetric or public-key encryption. In both schemes, two keys are involved, namely an encryption key and the corresponding decryption key. In the first scheme, symmetric encryption, knowing one of the two keys, either the encryption or the decryption key, enables one to determine with little or no effort the other key; consequently both keys must be kept secret. In the second scheme, the two keys are so fundamentally different that one of the two keys may be public without permitting users to compromise the security of the encryption scheme.

A2.A. Symmetric Encryption

Two operations are involved in virtually all symmetric cryptosystems, namely substitution and transposition. A substitution in its simplest form is a permutation of the alphabet. (We assume the same alphabet for the unencrypted data, called the plaintext, and for the encrypted data, called the ciphertext.) An example is the

APPENDIX

Caesar cipher, where each letter is replaced by the letter three positions farther in the alphabet. Decryption is simply the inverse of the substitution function. Given the original function, the inverse can be determined very easily.

While substitution is defined in terms of the characters of the underlying alphabet, transposition operates on the positions of the characters in the plaintext. In the simplest case, a transposition is simply a permutation of the characters in the plaintext; the result of applying this transposition to the plaintext is then a permutation of the plaintext. Again, decryption is trivial if we know the transposition; all we have to do is undo the change in the positons of the characters.

These schemes are quite insecure (i.e., can easily be broken), even when they are combined, because the probabilities of the letters in a text thus encrypted remain unchanged. These probabilities are quite distinct and vary from language to language. For example, the letter E occurs more often in a typical English text than the letter X or Q; thus even though E may be replaced by X or Q, the high probability with which that letter occurs will signal that it is the encryption of E. The information contained in those probabilities can be used to break the encryption scheme. In order to avoid this attack, a major goal of a good encryption scheme is to flatten the probabilities of the symbols in the underlying alphabet; in other words, one attempts to have every symbol occur equally often in the ciphertext, despite the fact that in the plaintext the frequency counts of different symbols will vary greatly.

An improvement is the Vigenère ciphers, where the substitution rule (i.e., the key) is a word or text and the encryption process changes each character depending on the character of the key in the same position. This scheme is one of the so-called polyalphabetic encryption schemes; in contrast to the previously discussed substitution schemes (which are monalphabetic, since a character is always replaced by the same character regardless of where in the text it appears), one and the same symbol may be mapped to different symbols, depending on where it appears in the plaintext.

When sufficient care is applied in the choice of the key, the cryptosecurity of the Vigenère ciphers is quite good. In fact, the only provably unbreakable cipher, the so-called one-time pad, is an extreme case of this cipher where the key is at least as long as the plaintext and is used exactly once. Decryption of Vigenère ciphers is again very easy if the encryption key is known, since it consists of subtracting the contribution of the key.

The commercially important Data Encryption Standard (DES) is a well-known example of a symmetric cryptosystem. It was proposed by the National Bureau of Standards in the mid-1970s and was implemented by IBM. This is a scheme in which blocks of 64 bits are en- and decrypted. The process is governed by a key with 56 bits (plus 8 additional bits for parity checks). Each 64-bit block is subject to 16 applications of nonlinear substitutions, alternating with transpositions. The DES is the object of a considerable controversy centering on Martin Hellman's accusation that the U.S. National Security Agency (NSA) had been involved in the choice of key length because a key length of 56 would enable the NSA to break the cipher with relatively little effort. Given the power of today's supercomputers (1989), the DES cannot be considered adequate any longer, except for very low-security communication.

A2.B. Asymmetric Encryption

Asymmetric or public-key cryptography is a fundamentally new approach to cryptography, outlined in the mid-1970s. We begin by stating the general idea, which is due to W. Diffie and M. E. Hellman. As before, we assume that the general en- and decryption schemes or algorithms are known and that the variable parts of our schemes are the keys. However, whereas before we had a situation where one key could easily be found when given the other key, now we assume that the two keys K for encryption and L for decryption are "substantially different". By this we mean that given one of the two keys

K_A and L_A of a particular user A, it is computationally infeasible to determine the other key.

We will call a problem computationally infeasible if it is one where a mathematical solution exists, but the fastest method for obtaining it would take far too long to be practical. For example, if it is known that the best solution for a problem of size n requires 2^{5n} steps ("size" being an abstract measure of the length of the input to the problem), it is quite irrelevant how fast we can perform one step; if n is large this problem is computationally infeasible. True, for smaller values of n, it is quite feasible to get a solution. For example, $n = 2$ we must execute 2^{10} or about 1000 steps. However, if $n = 20$, 2^{100} or about 10^{34} steps must be executed! Even if we can perform 100 steps in 1 ns it would still take approxiamelty 3000 trillion years! So, while mathematically a solution exists (for any value of n), computationally it is unattainable for larger values of n.

In a public-key cryptosystem, all users employ the same algorithms E for encryption and D for decryption. Each user A possesses a pair of keys K_A, L_A where K_A is A's encryption key to be used with E and L_A is A's decryption key to be used with D. The keys must satisfy the following relation:

$$D(E(M,K_A),L_A) = M \quad \text{for all messages M}$$

For technical reasons (mainly for digital signatures) we also assume that applications of the functions together with their two keys are interchangeable, i.e.,

$$E(D(M,L_A),K_A) = M \quad \text{for all messages M}$$

The central idea of public-key cryptography is that each user A places his encryption key K_A in a public file much like a telephone directory, while keeping the decryption key L_A secret. Thus every user has access to other users' encryption keys but knows only his own decryption key. This implies that a user A must communicate the key K_A in a secure way to the public file administrator; otherwise problems of authentication may arise.

Suppose now that another user B wants to send a message M to A in a confidential manner. User B looks up A's encryption key K_A in the public directory and sends A the following ciphertext:

$$C = E(M, K_A)$$

Note that this is possible since K_A is public. Now A applies his secret decryption key to the received ciphertext C,

$$D(C, L_A) = M$$

and thus retrieves the original message. Note that only A can perform this decryption process since by assumption only A knows L_A. Thus, the transmission of C can be understood only by the intended recipient.

There are two very important implications of this scheme:

1. If two users wish to communicate with each other, it is not necessary (in contrast to symmetric cryptosystems) that there be an initial exchange of keys between the participants in the communication. (This key exchange must of course occur via a secure channel.) Thus, it is not necessary that the participants in a secure exchange have had prior contact.

2. Only two keys are required for each user, independent of the total number of potential participants. This is in contrast to symmetric cryptosystems, where for n potential participants, in order to have secure communication between any two participants, a total of n $(n\text{-}1)$ keys is required. Here the analogy with the telephone system is instructive. In a certain sense, one can view the telephone number as a key. Clearly every participant has one public key which enables every other user to call that party. It is interesting to calculate what would happen if any two parties needed their own private key (telephone number) in order to be able to communicate (this is precisely the case for symmetric cryptosystems). If we had 1 million parties (telephones), we would require about a half trillion keys altogether! Thus the notion of public-key cryptography is significant.

Note that while nobody would actually call a million parties, the usefulness of the telephone system relies on the fact that we could call any one of the 1 million parties if we wished. The same applies to public-key cryptosystems.

In view of the fact that absolute security is practically unattainable, we settle for computational security; that is we assume that it is computationally (albeit not mathematically) infeasible to break the cipher. There are some obvious requirements which we must assume for any encryption scheme, asymmetric or not, namely that it permits speedy en- and decryption if the corresponding keys are available and that it flattens the probabilites of the different symbols in the alphabet. We must now also assume that determining the only secret piece in public-key cryptosystems, namely the decryption key L_A, is computationally infeasible, provided the two schemes D and E and the encryption key K_A are known. Finally, for such a scheme to be practical, it must be possible without undue effort to find pairs (K_A, L_A) for arbitrarily many users A.

The method outlined below satisfies all these requirements; it is due to Ronald Rivest, Adi Shamir, and Len Adleman, thence RSA scheme. The central underlying observation is the apparent discrepancy between the efforts required for solving two seeming closely related problems, namely testing whether a given integer is a prime number and factoring a given integer. Indeed, the best algorithm presently known will determine whether a given integer with d digits is a prime in time polynomial in d, while for factoring no polynomial time solution is known. While it is beyond the scope of this appendix to explain the time complexity of algorithms, the following example will put this in perspective. The test of whether a given integer with 200 (decimal) digits is a prime may require perhaps one minute of CPU time, but determining the prime factors of the same integer, perhaps after we determined that it is not a prime, could take many million years on the fastest computer currently available.

The RSA scheme is implemented as follows. One chooses a pair of s-digits primes p and q with s so large that factoring their product $n = p \cdot q$ is computationally infeasible (without knowing p or q). Furthermore, one chooses two integers d and e such that the conditions below hold:

1. The greatest common divisor of e and $(p - 1)(q - 1)$ is 1.

2. $e \cdot d = 1 \bmod[(p - 1)(q - 1)]$.

Encryption of a message M now proceeds as follows. M must be viewed as an integer between 0 and n-1 ($=p \cdot q$ -1); thus its length is to be no greater than 2s. The ciphertext C to be transmitted is then computed by

$$C = M^e \bmod (n)$$

In other words, the message is raised to the e th power, modulo n. This is of course again a number with no more than 2s digits. Decryption can be performed by subjecting the ciphertext C to the same operation, but now with the decryption exponent d:

$$M = C^d \bmod(n)$$

It follows from a number of theoretical considerations that this indeed yields the original message M. If our message is longer than the block length, we divide it into blocks of appropriate size and transmit each block separately enciphered.

A participant in this public-key cryptosystem would therefore have to determine first two s - digit primes. (Here is where we need the test for primality.) This would be followed by the determination of d and e, a computationally simple task. Then he would publish the product n of the two primes and e, but keep both prime factors of n, namely p and q, and the decryption exponent d secret. Factoring comes into play because knowing the prime factors of the public n enables one to determine d with little effort when given e. On the other hand, there is evidence that breaking this code is about as difficult as

112

factoring n. It should be noted, however, that we do not have a mathematical proof that factoring is difficult; all we know is that despite substantial efforts over the past centuries, no efficient algorithm is known.

We note that raising a number M to the e th power requires no more then $2 \log_2(e)$ multiplications. Although the time complexity of this operation is not linear in the length of n, encryption and decryption can still be considered efficient algorithms. At present, a length for n of 400 decimal digits ($s \geq 200$) appears very satisfactory; without an unprecedented breakthrough in the theory of factoring, there is no hope that factoring of such numbers would ever become feasible within our lifetime, even with the most breathtaking advances in computer technology.

A2.C. Selected Applications

A2.C.1. Data Integrity

It is clear that encryption does not prevent access to our data for the purpose of changing them. It does, however, allow us to detect whether subversion (replacing the original information by new and valid but unintended information) has occurred. Here is how this can be done, using redundancy and subsequent encryption.

Assume that we want to store a block B of information of length n in such a way that an attempt at replacing B with some other block B' is detected. Instead of storing B, we double B (i.e., consider B followed by another copy of B) and then encrypt this block of length $2n$, yielding the ciphertext C to be stored (see Fig. A4). It is important to observe that in C, it is not apparent that the original plaintext consisted of two identical halves. Thus, if someone were to replace C by some other C', it is very unlikely that C' would decrypt into a message (a different one since C' is different from C) which also consists of two identical halves. In fact, in this case the probability of someone (without knowing the encryption scheme) producing such a C' is $1/2^n$.

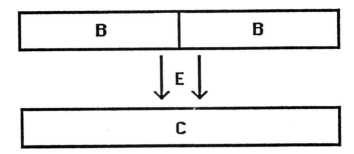

Figure A4.

A2.C.2. Authentication and Digital Signatures

The most immediate authentication problem is the log-on procedure for getting access to a computer system. The conventional methods employ passwords: the user sends the password and the system verifies the user's identity by comparing this password to the file of all valid passwords. Only if the transmitted password is found in the file will the user be granted access to the system. Given the fact that operating systems are notoriously unsafe, it is very possible that someone may obtain access to the file of all passwords. This very real danger can be avoided by storing only the encryption of the passwords but not the passwords themselves, and by encrypting each received password and comparing that encryption to the stored encryptions. However, this still leaves the possibility of an interception of the transmitted password.

An even more complicated situation exists with respect to digital signatures. Here we have all the previous problems, but in addition the signature must depend on the message which is to be signed. If this were not the case, one genuine signature could be reused for many forged messages. Note that the validity of handwritten signatures depends on the assumption that only the signer can produce that signature; in particular, one implicitly assumes that nobody can copy a (handwritten) signature. If a digital signature were merely a sequence of

0's and 1's which does not depend on the message to which it lends authentication, it could simply be cut off, duplicated, and attached to other messages. This is possible since it is trivial to make "perfect" copies of a string of 0's and 1's.

The general principle of authentication is to encrypt a rapidly changing unique value by using a previously agreed upon key. An outline of a possible authentication sequence from user B to user A follows. We assume a public-key cryptosystem; thus B knows A's encryption key K_A but nobody other than A knows A's decryption key L_A.

1. B sends to A in cleartext a rapidly changing unique value, e.g., the time of day as known to B.

2. A encrypts the received time of day using the secret key L_A and sends the resulting message to B.

3. B decrypts A's message using the public key K_A and compares the resulting plaintext with the time of day when B received that message. If there is no long delay, B is satisfied that A is the originator of the message.

We conclude by giving a scheme for producting digital signatures. Again we assume a public-key cryptosystem. Suppose A wants to send to B a signed message M. This can be achieved as follows:

A sends B the message

$$C = E(D(M,L_A),K_B)$$

where, as usual K_B is B's public encryption key and L_A is A's secret decryption key. B retrieves M from C by first decrypting C using B's private key L_B and then subjecting the resulting message to an encryption with A's public key K_A.

Clearly, B can be satisfied that this message came from A as only A knows L_A and can thus produce $D(M, L_A)$. Note that there is no "physical" signature, but the evidence that A and nobody else sent the message is compelling. In fact, by saving the transmitted message C, B can actually supply a proof that A sent M.

While this digital signature scheme relies on public-key cryptosystems, digital signatures can also be based on symmetric encryption. For this we refer to the literature.

A3. Write - Once Disks

Digital optical disks are a relatively new technology for storing data. The technical setup is as follows. Each disk is coated with a reflective metal such as tellurium. Reading and writing are performed using a laser. More specifically, reading involves determining the reflectivity of a given position on the disk, while writing consists of melting holes into the coating (at a higher power setting of the laser). Clearly, the holes' reflectivity is lower; holes correspond to 1's, whereas the higher reflectivity of the unadulterated coating represents 0's.

This setup has a number of important practical implications. The information density on digital optical disks can be much higher, as optical recording permits much finer "grain" than magnetic recording. Head crashes cannot occur, thereby increasing reliability. The material of the disks and their manufacture is simpler, thereby reducing the price. Finally, as a consequence of the technology once a 1 is written (i.e. a hole is burned into the coating), this 1 cannot be changed back into a 0. Thus, digital optical disks are write-once memory (other examples are punched card, paper tape, and PROM).

It is incorrect to conclude from the inability to change a 1 back to a 0 that information, once recorded, may not be updated. A simple example is the number 1, recorded in any of BCD, ASCII, or EBCDIC, which can in fact be changed into any of the numbers 3, 5, 7, or 9, without ever changing a 1 into a 0. Note that 0's can (and will, in this case!) be changed into 1's.

	BCD		ASCII		EBCDIC	
1	000	001	0101	0001	1111	0001
3	000	011	0101	0011	1111	0011
5	000	101	0101	0101	1111	0101
7	000	111	0101	0111	1111	0111
9	001	001	0101	1001	1111	1001

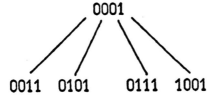

In fact, one can show considerably more. In an elegant paper [A1], Rivest and Shamir show that there exist codes with the property that any piece of information, stored in write-once memory, can be changed into any other desired piece of information using only the operation of changing 0's into 1's. In fact, such codes even exist if one wishes to update not just once, but t times, for $t \geq 1$. Furthermore, the cost (in length of the codewords) to be paid for this facility is relatively small. Rivest and Shamir show that in order to accommodate t writes (one original write and t-1 update), a fixed-length code must be at least of length $v \cdot t / \log(t)$ if 2^v symbols are to be represented ($t \geq 2$). Since clearly v is the minimal length of any fixed-length code for representing that many symbols, the cost is just $t / \log(t)$ asymptotically.

We assume the following scenario. We have a large amount of data which are to be stored on a digital optical disk in such a way that the data cannot be modified. The attacker is assumed to be able to change individual 0's to 1's. Contrary to the usual schemes designed for protecting against subversion, we require that even arbitrarily extensive modifications must be detected. Note that in most conventional schemes this condition is not satisfied. For example, error detecting codes will only work if at most a certain prespecified number of bits have been changed.

A3.A. **Immutable Codes**

A code C for our purposes is a finite set of finite strings (or words) over the alphabet $\{0,1\}$. If all strings in C are of the same length s, we write $C \subseteq \{0,1\}^s$ and call the code C a fixed-length code. We use C^* to denote the set (or language) of all strings which can be obtained by concatenating strings of C together. Clearly, a code C is of use only if any string C^* can be uniquely decoded, i.e., if:

$$x_1 \cdot \ldots \cdot x_m = y_1 \cdot \ldots \cdot y_n \text{ and } x_i, y_j \ \varepsilon \ C$$
$$\text{for } i=1, \ldots, m, j=1, \ldots, n \quad \text{imply}$$
$$m = n \text{ and } x_i = y_i \text{ for all } i=1,\ldots,n.$$

For each $v \ \varepsilon \ C$, v of length s, we define the set $\psi(v) \subseteq \{0,1\}^s$, as follows:

$$v \ \varepsilon \ \psi (v), \quad \text{and if } w = v_1 \cdot 0 \cdot v_2 \ \varepsilon \ \psi(v)$$
$$\text{then also } v_1 \cdot 1 \cdot v_2 \ \varepsilon \ \psi(v).$$

For example, if $v = 000$ then $\psi(v) = \{0,1\}^3$; if $v = 10110$, then $\psi(v) = \{10110, 10111, 11110, 11111\}$. Informally, $\psi(v)$ is the set of all words obtained from v by replacing zero or more 0's by 1's.

A code C is called immutable if for all $x_i, y_j \ \varepsilon C$, $i=1, \cdots$, $m, j=1, \cdots, n$,

$$y_1 \cdot \ldots \cdot y_n \ \varepsilon \ \psi(x_1) \cdot \ldots \cdot \psi(x_m) \quad \text{implies}$$

$$m = n \text{ and } x_i = y_i \quad \text{for all } i = 1, \ldots, n.$$

Informally, C is called immutable if for all strings $w = x_1 \cdot \ldots \cdot x_m$, $x_i \ \varepsilon \ C$, replacing one or more 0's in w by 1's will not result in a decodable string.

Proposition 1: Any subset of an immutable code is again immutable code.

1) Fixed-Length Immutable Codes: we define the fixed-length code IC_n as follows. Let k be the smallest integer such that

$$[M(k) :=] \binom{k}{k//2} \geq n$$

$$\text{where } k//2 = \begin{cases} k/2 & \text{if } k \text{ is even} \\ (k+1)/2 & \text{if } k \text{ is odd} \end{cases}$$

Then IC_n is that subset of $\{0,1\}^k$ which consists of all words with $k//2$ 0's.

Propositon 2: IC_n is an immutable code of cardinality at least n.

The fixed-length immutable code IC_n is "best" in the following sense.

Theorem 1: for all $k \geq 2$, there is no fixed-length immutable code of length k with more than $M(k)$ elements; IC_n is an optimal fixed-length immutable code.

It follows that compared to the shortest conventional fixed-length codes (simple binary codes), optimal fixed-length immutable codes require about $ln(s)$ additional bits.

2) Variable-Length Immutable Codes: it might appear initially that the ability to change any 0 into a 1 precludes the existence of variable-length immutable codes. This is incorrect; there are in fact, variable-length immutable codes. For examples of variable-length immutable codes, we refer to the literature.

A3.B. Alternative Schemes

While immutable codes are quite effective if data integrity is of concern, they do have the disadvantage that one must change the encoding of the data. This may be undesirable or unacceptable for various reasons. One obstacle might be that in order to represent, say, 128 or 256 different symbols (one byte in conventional encoding), the codewords of an optimal immutable code would be of length 10 or 12. In a byte-oriented environment, this means essentially using two bytes instead of one. Also, it may be desirable to stay with the conventional codes, namely BCD, ASCII, EBCDIC, for reasons external to the storage system.

1) Split Storage: split storage requires storing the data twice in different locations. However, in order to guarantee integrity on write-once media, we store the information once in one location using whatever code we wish to employ, and then we store the 1's complement of this message in another location. To see that this scheme guarantees data integrity one need only observe that every 0 in the original data must correspond to a 1 in the complemented data, and every 1 in the original data must correspond to a 0 in the complemented data. Thus, any attempt to change a 0 to 1 somewhere (either in the original or in the complemented data) will immediately be detected when the two are compared. Clearly, this scheme requires twice as much storage. However, on the one hand, in a byte-oriented environment, that much space might also be used by optimal fixed-length immutable codes, and on the other hand, this scheme has some rather interesting consequences. It is, for example, now possible to use any code, in particular the conventional codes such as BCD, ASCII, or EBCDIC can be used. More importantly, we may use (optimal variable-length) Huffman codes.

One attractive way of implementing this scheme is to write the 1's complement of a byte immediately after that byte. This method works well for fixed-length codes which require a complete byte or word (or multiple thereof), such as BCD, ASCII, or EBCDIC.

Note that in order to read the data in this case, no decoding is necessary (simply read from that half which is in clear text); only for ascertaining the data integrity the two halves must be compared.

2) Conventional Storage with Control Key: all preceding schemes require a relatively large amount of additonal space. In particular, optimal immutable codes require about $ln(s)$ + $O(1)$ additional bits to represent symbols conventionally represented by s bits. If $s = 8$ (i.e., one byte per symbol), three additional bits amount to an increase in space of almost 40 percent. Even if we use only two additional bits (this permits to represent just 252

instead of 256 [$=2^8$] symbols), the increase is still 25 percent. This may be unacceptable. Thus, less expensive schemes may also be of interest.

a) Control key schemes for guaranteed integrity: in this scheme, we store the data in any desired format. We also compute a control key and store it in such a way that data and control key form a unique pair, i.e., any possible change in either one of them would necessitate a change in the other one which is not possible. One easy and very direct way is to use immutable codes for the control key. In this case, the control key must only guarantee that any change in the data invalidates the control key. The function of the control key is to guarantee that the data have not been tampered with. Thus it serves as certificate of data integrity. Clearly, the control key should be significantly shorter than the data.

Note that it is crucial that data and control key form a unique pair. Otherwise, it may be possible to subvert the information and the control key (changing 0's to 1's) in such a way that the subversions can not be detected. Consequently, great care should be applied when choosing a particular scheme as the following two examples illustrate.

Example 1: assume that we use as control key the number of 1's in our data. In this case it is crucial to store the control key immutable. To see that otherwise the integrity of our data would not be guaranteed, consider the data 1234 stored in BCD,

$$000\ 001\ 000\ 010\ 000\ 011\ 000\ 100$$

and assume that we store the control key, namely the number of 1's (5), in BCD as well. Thus, our control key is

$$000\ 101\ .$$

Now consider the following subversion. Change the fifth position of the control key to 1 and at the same time change the fourth and fifth position (of the first word) of the data to 1's. Thus, we have data: 000 111 000 010 000 011 000 100 control key: 000 111 and one can easily see that no subversion can be detected. Consequently, the original pair consisting of data and control key was not a unique pair.

Example 2: let us take almost the same approach as in the first example, except now we have as control key the number of 0's. In this case it is possible to store the control key in any of BCD, ASCII, EBCDIC, or simple binary. This is because now data and key do form a unique pair. In fact, this holds for any representation $R(n)$ of the number n of 0's in the data, provided it satisfies the following condition. For every $n \geq 1$, changing one or more 0's into 1's in $R(n)$ will result either in a string which does not represent any number (this is usually the case for immutable codes) or it will result in a string which represents a number larger than n. Since any possible change in the data will decrease the number of 0's, but the only changes in the control keys which this scenario permits are changes resulting in the representation of larger numbers, data and control key form a unique pair. The integrity of our data is guaranteed.

Control key schemes usually require significantly less storage than direct encoding using immutable codes. If we have n data items, each represented with s bits, the required amount of additional space is bounded from below by $\log(s \cdot n)$ bits (Example 2 with simple binary storing of key). Using immutable codes for the control key will require slightly more additonal space, namely

$$\log(s \cdot n) + ln(\log(s \cdot n)) + O(1)$$

bits. Directly encoding the data with immutable codes on the other hand would require about $n \cdot ln(s)$ additional bits, which is significantly more than what is required by control key schemes.

Disadvantages of control key schemes: the disadvantage of all control key methods is that it is no longer possible to pinpoint precisely where subversion occurred. All that one can determine is whether the data set was modified or not. This may be totally inadequate for certain applications. For example, if individual data items in a database are to be used directly (as they usually are), ascertaining data integrity would require reading the complete data set. Thus, a (relatively small) saving of space translates into a tremendous loss of time.

Granularity tradeoff: this observation gives rise to a tradeoff. The data set is segmented and each segment has its own control key. The size of the segment is the vital parameter in this approach. This parameter has a rather wide range. One extreme is having just one segment for the whole data set; this requires the least amount of additional space, but usually much more time for ascertaining integrity. The other extreme is treating each byte as a segment; this requires the largest amount of additional space, but very little time for determining whether the data have been subverted.

Reference

[A1]   R.L. Rivest and A. Shamir, "How to re-use a 'write-one' memory," in *Proc. 14th Annu. Ass. Comput. Mach. Symp. on Theory of Computing*, May 5-7, 1982, pp. 105-113.

A4. Bibliographic Notes

The sections on Authorization Systems and on Cryptography are abridged from [60] (see also [58]), the section on write-once disks is condensed from [59].

Bibliography

[1]   F. Cohen: Computer Viruses - Theory and Experiments, DoD/NBS Seventh Conference on Computer Security, Proc. IFIP-SEC, 1984.

[2]   F. Cohen: Computer Viruses - Theory and Experiments, Computers and Security 6, 1987, 22-35.

[3]   F. Cohen: On the Implications of Computer Viruses and Methods of Defense, Computers and Security 7, 1988, 167-184.

[4]   The Wall Street Journal: Spreading a Virus, Nov. 7, 1988, pp. 1, 18.

[5]   D. Stipp, P. B. Carroll: A Little Mistake and a Virus Prodigy Got Quick Notoriety, The Wall Street Journal, Nov. 7, 1988, p. 18.

[6]   B. R. Schlender: Computer Security Firms Suggest Ways to Stop Viruses, The Wall Street Journal, Nov. 7, 1988, p. B3.

[7]   B. R. Schlender: Computer "Virus", Infiltrating Network, Shuts Down Computers Around the World, The Wall Street Journal, Nov. 4, 1988, p. B4.

[8]   J. Markoff: Virus in Military Computers Disrupts Systems Nationwide, The New York Times, Nov. 4, 1988, pp. 1,13.

[9]   S. Vogel: Disease of the Year: Illness as Glitch, Discover, January 1989, 664-66.

[10]   I. Peterson: Worming into a Computer's Vulnerable Core, Science News, Vol. 134, p. 310.

[11] J. Schwartz, R. Sanza: Big Bucks for Virus Killers, Newsweek, Nov. 28, 1988, p. 82.

[12] Program Notes: Virtually a Virus, But for a Good Cause, IEEE Spectrum, June 1989, p. 18.

[13] Houston Chronicle: Computer Threat Costly, Disruptive, June 5, 1988, Section 1, p. 11.

[14] Houston Chronicle: Computer 'Virus' Eats Information at NASA, July 5, 1988, Section 1, p. 4.

[15] J. Voelcker: Spread of Computer Viruses Worries Users, The Institute, IEEE, Vol. 12, No. 6, June 1988, pp. 1,9.

[16] B. Reid: Reflections on Some Recent Widespread Computer Break-Ins, CACM, Vol. 30, Feb. 1987, 103-105.

[17] ACM Forum: Letters to the Editor, CACM, Vol. 30, July 1987, 584-585.

[18] B. Kocher: President's Letter, CACM, Jan. 1989.

[19] D. H. Grendin: On Viruses, Forum, CACM, Vol. 32, May 1989, 541-543.

[20] ACM Forum: Letters to the Editor, CACM, Vol. 32, June 1989, 672-674.

[21] Business Bulletin: As Computer Virus Fears Grow, Insurers Focus on the Coverage Question, The Wall Street Journal, June 1, 1989, p.

[22] P. Samuelson: Can Hackers Be Sued for Damages Caused by Computer Viruses, CACM, Vol. 32, June 1989, 666-669.

[23] M. Gemignani: Viruses and the Criminal Law, CACM, Vol. 32, June 1989, 669-671.

[24] News Track: Unlucky Day in U.K. and U.S.A., CACM, Vol. 32, March 1989, p. 286.

[25] J. F. Smith: European "Hacker" Spies Top Secret U.S. Computers, USA Today, March 3, 1989, p. 6A.

[26] S. Wilcox: Criminal Investigation Launched After Virus Infects Internet, IEEE Computer, Dec. 1988, p. 81.

[27] News Track: Slap on the Wrist, CACM, Vol. 32, May 1989, p. 534.

[28] Transition: Suspended, Newsweek, June 5, 1989, p. 61.

[29] T. Eisenberg, D. Gries, J. Hartmanis, D. Holcomb, M. S. Lynn, T. Santoro: The Cornell Commission: On Morris and the Worm, CACM, Vol. 32, June 1989, 706-709.

[30] J. R. Wilke: Student Indicted on Charge Linked to Computer Virus, The Wall Street Journal, July 27, 1989, p. B2.

[31] J. F. Shoch, J. A. Hupp: The "Worm" Programs - Early Experience with a Distributed Computation, CACM, Vol. 25, March 1982, 172-180.

[32] A. K. Dewdney: Computer Recreations, Scientific American 250 (5), 1984, 14-22.

[33] A. K. Dewdney: Computer Recreations, Scientific American 252 (3), 1985, 14-23.

[34] D. G. Jones, A. K. Dewdney: Core Ware Guidelines, Department of Computer Science, University of Western Ontario, 1984.

[35] H. J. Highland: Computer Viruses - A Post Mortem, Computers and Security 7, 1988, 117-125.

[36] W. H. Murray: The Application of Epidemiology to Computer Viruses, Computers and Security 7, 1988, 139-145.

[37] M. W. Eichin, J. A. Rochlis: With Microscope and Tweezers: An Analysis of the Internet Virus of November 1988, MIT Internal Report, 1989.

[38] K. Thompson: Reflections on Trusting Trust, CACM, Vol. 27, Aug. 1984, 761-763.

[39] E. H. Spafford: Crisis and Aftermath, CACM, Vol. 32, June 1989, 678-687.

[40] D. Seeley: Password Cracking: A Game of Wits, CACM, Vol. 32, June 1989, 700-703.

[41] P. J. Brusil, D. P. Stokesberry: Towards a Unified Theory of Managing Large Network, IEEE Spectrum, April 1989, 39-42.

[42] H. J. Highland: Anatomy of a Virus Attack, Computers and Security 7, 1988, 145-150.

[43] C. Stoll: Stalking the Wiley Hacker, CACM, Vol. 31, May 1988, 484-497.

[44] News Track: Wiley Hacker, the Sequel, CACM, Vol. 32, April 1989, p. 417.

[45] B. Kocher: President's Letter, CACM, Vol. 32, June 1989.

[46] News Track: Death of a Hacker, CACM, Vol. 32, August 1989, p. 916.

[47] H. J. Highland: An Overview of 18 Virus Protection Products, Computers and Security 7, 1988, 157-161.

BIBLIOGRAPHY

[48] H. J. Highland: Data Physician - A Virus Protection Program, Computers and Security 6, 1987, 73-79.

[49] E. L. Leiss: Authorization Systems with Bounded Propagation, Proc. 18th Annual Allerton Conf. on Communication, Control, and Computing, Montecello, IL, Oct. 1980, 491-496.

[50] E. L. Leiss, C. Jitmedha: Horizontally and Vertically Bounded Propagation of Privileges, Information Processing Letters 22, 1986, 319-327.

[51] J. Paredaens, F. Ponsaert: Grant Levels in an Authorization Mechanism, Information Processing Letters 11 (4,5), 1980, 152-155.

[52] R. L. Routh: A Proposal for an Architectural Approach which Apparently Solves All Known Software-Based Internal Computer Security Problems, Operating Systems Review 18 (3), 1984, 31-39.

[53] F. G. F. Davis, R. E. Gantenbein: Recovering from a Computer Virus Attack, J. Systems and Software 7, 1987, 253-258.

[54] Virus Defense Alert, Computers and Security 7, 1988, 156-163.

[55] H. J. Highland: How to Combat a Computer Virus, Computers and Security 7, 1988, pp. 157, 161, 162.

[56] V. Fak: Are We Vulnerable to a Virus Attack? Computers and Security 7, 1988, 151-155.

[57] M. M. Pozzo, T. E. Gray: An Approach to Containing Computer Viruses, Computers and Security 6, 1987, 321-331.

[58] E. L. Leiss: Principles of Data Security, Plenum Publishing Corp., New York, NY, 1982.

[59] E. L. Leiss: Data Integrity in Digital Optical Disks, IEEE Trans. Computers, Vol. C-33, No. 9, 1984, 818-827.

[60] E. L. Leiss: Data Security, in Encyclopedia of Physical Science and Technology (ed. R. A. Meyers), Vol. 4, Academic Press, 106-124.

Index